World Weary Woman

Marie-Louise von Franz, Honorary Patron

Studies in Jungian Psychology by Jungian Analysts

Daryl Sharp, General Editor

WORLD WEARY WOMAN

Her Wound and Transformation

CARA BARKER

Canadian Cataloguing in Publication Data

Barker, Cara
World weary woman: her wound and transformation

(Studies in Jungian psychology by Jungian analysts; 96)

Includes bibliographical references and index.

ISBN 0-919123-97-X

1. Suffering.
2. Individuation (Psychology)
3. Women—Psychology
4. Jungian psychology.
I. Title. II. Series.

BF789.S8B37 2001 155.9'3 C00-933183-2

INNER CITY BOOKS
Box 1271, Station Q
Toronto, ON M4T 2P4, Canada

Telephone (416) 927-0355 / Fax (416) 924-1814
E-mail: icb@inforamp.net / Web site: www.innercitybooks.net

Honorary Patron: Marie-Louise von Franz.
Publisher and General Editor: Daryl Sharp.
Senior Editor: Victoria Cowan.

INNER CITY BOOKS was founded in 1980 to promote the understanding and practical application of the work of C.G. Jung.

Cover:"Untitled," relief print by Vicki Cowan.

Printed and bound in Canada by University of Toronto Press Incorporated

CONTENTS

See final pages for descriptions of other Inner City Books

Acknowledgments

None of these pages would have been written without the original impetus and urging of my son, Matthew Ryan Foster, and the events that happened through his death; my daughter, Brandy, and her encouragement; and the many women who took part in this journey into the inner terrain of soul.

At every juncture, when my doubt and frustration mounted, others offered unsolicited encouragement. I am indebted to Sir Laurens van der Post, Helen Luke, Marion Woodman, Gregg Furth, Elisabeth Kubler-Ross, Larry Dossey, Natalie Goldberg, Jacob Goering, Hermann Strobel, Diane Cousineau Brutsche, Vicki Heland, Daryl Sharp and Vicki Cowan. Without the support and practical assistance of my analysts, the research committee, and the faculty of the C.G. Jung Institute in Kusnacht, Switzerland, the labor and delivery would have done me in. This work was also moved forward by the interest of all the World Weary People along the labyrinth: support group attendees, students, professionals and colleagues at the Institute for Noetic Sciences, The American Cancer Society, MADD, Johns Hopkins University, the University of Maryland, Georgetown University, Arizona State University, Compassionate Friends, and many hospice organizations, schools and churches.

I am indebted especially to those who shared their stories and so generously gave their permission to include them here.

I voyaged on this tempestuous sea for almost twenty years. It is one of the most painful lives, I think, that one can imagine; for neither did I enjoy God, nor did I find happiness in the world. When I was experiencing the enjoyments of the world, I felt sorrow when I recalled what I owed to God. When I was with God, my attachments to the world disturbed me. This was a war so troublesome that I don't know how I was able to suffer it even a month, much less for so many years.

—Teresa of Avila, *The Book of Her Life.*

I've always said that there are two great sources of corruption in life, corruption by power, and corruption by suffering. We have got to hold out against powerful men and societies who dominate vulnerable and less-powerful people—and other forms of life. And we must take an equally strong stand against becoming bitter, and vengeful, and cynical, and even anarchical because of what others have inflicted on us. . . . It is the hallmark of a truly integrated person that he will not allow his suffering to turn him sour.

—Sir Laurens van der Post (in conversation).

Preface

That a story has a beginning, middle and end is no surprise, but there is still a challenge in discovering how best to tell it. My personal struggle is how to speak about the connection between the suffering of a particular kind of person—referred to here as World Weary Woman—and her redemption, in those mysterious ways which reinstill the sacred into the profane.

Too frequently, what is sacred for a single individual is reduced to a prescriptive panacea for the many. What this overlooks is one simple fact: we heal as individual human beings. We have names, addresses and souls. What is good for one may be toxic to another. Our allergies are different, as are our antidotes.

The task is discernment—for those who suffer, those who write, and those who suffer writing. The person who knows misery must sort out who she is from who she is not. She must awaken to the peculiarities of her own situation, setting it apart from, as well as connecting it with, the predicaments of others in her community. The redemptive process requires reverence for one's own nature. Those called to this work discover that they do well to notice the particular details that make their story their own.

This is the task of individuation: to differentiate ourselves from the herd and take what is discovered and put it to use for the greater good, in practical ways. Paradoxically, by becoming aware of what makes us unique, we discover our connection. But this is not a connection that produces anonymity. Rather, it values what distinguishes each of us from others. How nature develops our bodies illustrates the point. We cannot have a functioning body unless we have differentiated cells comprising the various muscles, bones, tissues, nerves and vasculature. Differentiation has nothing to do with a value judgment of good or bad. A liver cell is neither better nor worse than a brain cell; both are necessary. We cannot develop into creatures of greater consciousness and collaboration without distinguishing one life form from another.

Just as I was tempted to forget the importance of individual differences, a reminder came that haunted me. Ten years ago, I completed a research project involving adults known in the literature as Type A women. I had drawn conclusions and presented the findings to my committee. Assuming

I was finished, I put the matter aside with a smug intellectual finality. But, as we are told, "Pride goeth before a fall . . ."

Within months, remnants of their stories came back with a vengeance. Facing my own fresh ordeal, the loss of my son, I discovered that I had lost my way in the abyss. Searching for the thread that might help me find a way through my predicament, I turned to communities designed to help those who suffered similar circumstances. I was stunned by the variation of responses to the experience of losing children. Despite the similarities in our stories, there were also differences, some of which left us unconnected to one another.

Ironically, it was rarely other bereaved parents that made the crucial difference in my own reconciliation with loss. Again and again, it was the unsolicited reaching out of the women who had so generously shared their stories in the research project. They were the ones who touched me profoundly. As they learned of my loss, over time and without exception, they reached out in uncommon ways, especially considering that only one of them had lost a child. However, each knew firsthand the experience of losing in her own childhood someone or something that was treasured. Sensitized to the inner experience of those losses, they connected in ways I would not have dreamt possible at the time of our co-research.

During that period I had no idea of the importance of their capacity for self-discovery. This was the essential quality present in every person that made such a difference in helping me navigate the waters of my own suffering. Those most helpful seemed to have a deep, abiding appreciation for entering what's real, regardless the cost. They were able to engage with the Mystery.

Our ancestors' ancestors knew the importance of entering the Unknown with heart, senses and mind wide open. Without books, recipes or reference points, they were at the zero point. When something unexpected happened, including anything that threatened security, our earliest grandmothers and grandfathers had to validate their own experience. They had to trust their connection to the experience, course-correcting their relationship to their world accordingly. Without doing so, they could not survive.

From earliest times, Story has provided a connection with Meaning. Our ancestors' stories came from hardship and their creations, from the disparity between what their hearts cherished and what was missing. Discovering through difficulties what it means to suffer the human condition of soulful yearning, stories grew, seeking containers. From the beginning, death has come from life; life has followed death. The two are part of the same story. Where something was lost, something was found.

Vehicles through which to do the telling varied, depending upon availability and message. Sometimes it was primitive markings on cave walls. Sometimes, what spirit needed to be recorded was done through song, dance, instrument or invention. The movement of human consciousness that comes from suffering what it means to be human has always required expression. Through sounds, shapes, pictures, movement or clay, humankind struggled to leave its mark. Regardless of the material, the message is but a variation on a universal theme: "This is what I've found. This is who I am. This is what I have discovered about what it means to be human." Whether we like it or not, most of what we can offer from our hand and footprints comes from times of suffering and deliverance.

In the following pages I make no attempt to discuss the redemptive journey through suffering from either an academic or theological perspective. Neither training nor experience qualify me in these arenas. Perhaps, in the end, all we can ever really share is our own firsthand experience. At least that is how it was for me. I felt suffocated by what Westerners refer to as the "information highway." It was not the voice of the masses that helped, it was intimacy with what was happening closest to me, inside and out. More than anything, I needed a big dose of what my mother used to call "peace and quiet." What supported the endeavor was not advice or other people's opinions. What was useful was hearing how my predicament fit in the cosmos—where humankind has faced difficulty since the beginning of time, how the experience lives on in World Weary People today, in all its forms. This is nothing short of an art that lives within us all, whether we've discovered its unique form or not.

When her suffering is greatest, World Weary Woman finds she must give it voice so that her pain does not turn back upon her in further destruction. There is a healing power in creative expression. Throughout my own process I was reminded of this fact. Moments after the phone call telling me of my son's accident, I found myself hurling all sorts of things into the suitcase: toiletries, nightgown, change of clothes. This is not surprising. What did surprise me, however, was the inclusion of another kind of survival kit: an empty journal for dreams and drawings and a set of colored pencils. Logically, there was no rhyme nor reason to the "basics" from my closet. I was too dazed for any plan. But instinctually, the deepest part of me knew the essentials: creative materials to express what would be too toxic to contain, even if I had no words to verbalize what I felt. It turned out to be these very raw materials that held the rawness no other human being could hold for or with me at the time.

What follows is an impression, based on observations of World Weary Woman and her archetypal story, coupled with my own.

Introduction
An Adventure in Creative Living

For as long as I can remember, I have been fascinated with what I've come to call *creative living*. When chaos comes unforeseen, why is it that some respond and create vibrantly from it, while others retreat, stiffen and wither in the field of possibilities? And, how can we know who will do which? How can we predict what we ourselves will do when what is beyond our control breaks through the walls of our little dwelling and threatens to ruin everything we've struggled for?

Perhaps the answer will never be entirely known. The key is in the asking. To do so requires a continual reintegration of the "me" I've come to believe I am with what is natural. But then, as a dream figure once reminded me: "What is Eternal is under constant revision." As I grow older, what endures holds increasingly more meaning than that which turns to dust. In fact, the answer matters less to me than the process of holding the question: What does creative living require of me today?

More times than I can count, what I've begun with industry has taken on a direction I did not plan. Whatever I thought my efforts were spinning shifted the instant there was an opening for the unpredictable to enter.

So it was with the following pages. What I originally believed I was producing, more than ten years ago, is entirely different from the book you now hold in your hand. The original thread has not wavered, although I have dropped or misplaced it many times. But in the process of relocating its "spindle" (a symbol used in what follows), I have been met by the reality which poets, mystics and artists have known forever: while I may be spinning, it is the Old Woman at the wheel, the one I cannot see, who sets the course, the story, into motion.

My part is to make room, give time, devote myself to coming together in greater harmony with what the Old Woman sends my way through her spinning wheel of Fate. The hope is an increasing consciousness concerning how best to live creatively with the particularities of the thread she's sent my way.

Accepting such an endeavor moves us into the domain of the sacred. For such an effort means that we consecrate our way of living—dedicating what is created through us to some meaningful purpose. Perhaps the attempt to do so brings us back to the necessity of sacred suffering: making each day an offering, paying homage to what transcends our limited understanding of why we are here. Discovering that to do otherwise leaves our soul wounded, whimpering, withering, we face the fact that if our condition is to change, we must make a leap of faith.

But we are not the first, and we are not alone. As we are reminded through the stories of other people, there are those who have gone before.

1
The World Weary Woman Study

A Foot in Two Worlds

This book is the result of a ten-year study that aimed to discover what it means for a particular kind of woman to be human: an intention of self-discovery. At the outset, the investigation seemed rational. But once I extricated myself from the library, the process took an unexpected turn. I entered the land of the irrational: the terrain of the feminine way. Anything but linear, the pursuit has challenged me to move with one foot in the instinctual body while the other moves in the world of word.

I had no idea the study would span a decade. The easier path would have been a shorter, more limited, "traditional" research project. I argued my case. I fought what seemed too difficult. I protested that what was asked from places deeper than my brain was unnecessary, or could be postponed. But the part of me I had not met pushed in the most persistent way for the birth of this baby until my resistance gave way and I surrendered to the authority of a central force within. My job has been to learn when to work, when to relax and let nature take its course, and to remember, no matter where I was in the process (or "it" was in me), to breathe.

Learning to breathe deeply, to take what comes in a relaxed way, has become a soul imperative. Otherwise, I cannot attend World Weary Ones, those of all ages who endure a common syndrome. At times when the weight of the world's demands is too much, each complains of feeling suffocated, compressed or breathless. During these periods they feel cut off from their own creative spirit, a spirit requiring that what has grown dry find moisture once more.

Format, Process and Population

This book describes World Weary Folks who come forward for assistance. However, the reason for doing the study was not the same as the reason for now sharing it with you. Always a fan of Agatha Christie mysteries, I found myself reviewing clues that came during the data-gathering phase of the research project on major life changes. When unexpected twists and turns of fate entered the lives of the co-researchers and myself, something in me remembered a little image or vignette that one of these women had shared during our investigation that seemed helpful to one or both of us. Often, the woman expressed surprise. "You remember my drawings so well—and I've forgotten about them!" But increasingly, especially for those who have begun their own depth work journey, which Jung called assisted individuation, we find solace, hints and guidance from the expressive work of those who, for the most part, identify themselves as "artistically challenged." Together we stand in endless awe, witnessing the unconscious at work. As it sends forth its healing imagery, we are reminded that we are receiving documents from the soul. That these hieroglyphs of self-expression are not taken seriously in our time reflects how far we've wandered from the Mysteries that redeem and heal our hurt.

The reason for presenting this material on the threshold of the twenty-first century is that, although the findings may be peculiar to the temperament and circumstances of high performance women, sharing the process of our unfolding context may be helpful to anyone.

Initially, the method was: 1) to interview self-selected women, known in the literature as Type A, regarding their perceptions; 2) to record past and future impressions of each regarding the development of her personality through the incorporation of drawing; and 3) to determine whether there were any unifying threads that might be archetypal.

The focus was to find out what we could about influences on the development of their personalities. The most frequent self-descriptions were "driven" and "high performance." Those who have so generously served as co-participants then and now, I refer to here as the Original Eight. But as noted in chapter two, the process has been so organic that the population of contributors has grown. In addition to the Original Eight, twenty-eight other women, having heard of the study, offered to contribute anonymously. Eleven of this number described losses in the past ten years necessitating reconstruction of their self-concept—suffering involving one or more losses through death or dissolution of a significant relationship, or changes involving health, home, career or financial security. Seventeen of the thirty-six suffered the loss of a child.

The total population drawn upon in the ten-year follow-up presented to the C.G. Jung Institute in Switzerland numbered thirty-six, referred to collectively as "World Weary Woman." However, not a day passes in my consulting room or travels when I am not impressed with the rampantly growing incidence of the syndrome at virtually any age.

At times, "she," as World Weary Woman, refers to the composite of all thirty-six stories when what is said was voiced as a major theme. At other times, her voice breaks out through the unique words of a participant whose language captures the essence, even though the specifics vary greatly. World Weary Woman becomes a complex portrait with ever-changing features. For example, the Original Eight are not the same women psychologically, physically or spiritually as they were ten years ago. Although they tested out as Type A when younger, with more years and experience they have softened as they engage in the second stage of life. As World Weary Woman becomes more seasoned, the need for achievement seems in flux.[1] She, too, is a paradox. As the unknown entered the study, methodology had to accommodate the unconventional. This meant creating a heuristic study. According to Douglass and Moustakas:

> In its purest form, heuristics is a passionate and discerning personal involvement in problem solving, an effort to know the essence of some aspect of life through the internal pathways of the self. . . . When a passionate, disciplined commitment is brought into the search to illuminate a question or to discover a solution to a problem, heuristic research has fulfilled the first vital step. The data that emerge are autobiographical, original, and accurately descriptive of the textures and structures of lived experience.[2]

Giorgi expressed what I wanted to achieve:

> [To] do justice to the lived aspects of human phenomena, one first has to know how someone actually experienced what has been lived. This means that a description becomes necessary when it is possible to get one.[3]

Since I had begun my own Jungian analysis some time before the onset of the project, it was easy to find parallels between the two. The meaning of heuristics is "to find out or to discover," taking its root from the Greek word *heuretikos,* defined more personally as "I find." It evolved, as did

---

[1] This matches developmental studies of Type A people, although the literature makes no commentary on such a dynamic.

[2] In "Heuristic Inquiry: The Internal Search To Know," p. 39.

[3] Ibid., p. 94.

Jung's exploration of individuation, through the philosophical tradition which encouraged the individual to turn within, listen to what was there, and learn from it. In fact, the process seemed remarkably close to what I was experiencing in analysis.

The role of analyst, heuristic researcher and artist seemed related. Douglass and Moustakas illustrate this:

> Just as the artist must control the use of color and shading in painting a sunset, so must the heuristic inquirer discipline the quest for knowledge in precise and exact terms. When to probe deeper, when to shift the focus, when to pause to examine inmost layers of meaning, when to reflect, when to describe—all are considerations of timing and attunement that demand a disciplined sensitivity of the nature and essence of an experience if it is to be revealed.[4]

This meant our task was to immerse ourselves in our experience, to acquire what we could from it, and to make sufficient space for conscious realization of the meaning. Together, we had come full circle.

At the culmination of the project in December of 1990, faculty and colleagues who reviewed the research urged me to publish the results. They insisted that the information applied to themselves and/or loved ones and was useful. But I was ambivalent. I had finished it, yet something seemed incomplete. I had the vague feeling that there was a deeper context for the story that emerged, but what was it? The piece gathered dust on my desk for the next few weeks.

One month later, necessity forced me to submerge myself in another unexpected spiral of life. I could not escape the need for major surgery—two days before my forty-fifth birthday. Ironically, the moment before I went under anesthesia, I wondered, if my life were over, what had I failed to express, write, paint? This surprised me. I would not have guessed that at a moment of confronting my mortality, I would question my creativity. Consequently, part of my post-operative course involved the exploration of the experience through ink and paint. The pursuit has not subsided.

Just when I thought I had completed this process of circling down into my embodied experience of loss, something more challenging arose, yanking me down into deeper waters. On March 21, 1991, a phone call came that changed my life, challenging what I was learning from the research

---

[4] Ibid., p. 41.

more deeply than I could appreciate at the time. My only son had been killed.

Grieving the loss brought countless surprises, tortures and blessings, and a persistent sense that a story existed which could help me in a time of raging chaos. It took some time to find it—in the Grimm collection of fairy tales. When I found "Mother Holle," I knew I was not alone. What I experienced seemed part of a larger, archetypal story. Although the particulars might vary, there appeared to be a unifying thread which reconnects us to redemption. I was reminded through the imagery of "Mother Holle" and related narratives that transformation can come through suffering the sort of loss which lacks all apparent meaning. In the face of the worst a mother can imagine, transformation is possible, for choice exists.

As imagery from my unconscious gathered, I began to notice something. One level of the well of my creative imagination was personal. It offered memories of good and painful times between my son and me, as well as recollections of other personal losses and traumas I had experienced from childhood on.

But there was also a deeper source of these healing images, and that was from a substratum that seemed collective. In hindsight, when studying the Jungian literature, what I found is obvious. How often are we told that the unconscious consists of personal and impersonal content? In truth, experiencing this for myself in the context of my suffering brought that reality to life in a way that books could not.

As these images began to collide and coincide, a realization dawned. A connection was forming with "Mother Holle" which, as you will later see, became increasingly useful.

Interpersonal Reconnections

As women in the initial study learned of my loss, each contacted me of her own accord, in her own unique way. For some inexplicable reason, it seemed important that they answer the call to reconnect. At the time, I thought nothing of it, but was moved by their outreach. As I circled downward in this unwanted spin of my life's wheel, a number of these women became a special source of support.

In one way, the depths of their sympathy and empathy might be surprising. But as I reviewed the original transcription of their own stories, I sensed something else at play. Their support reflected their own sensitivity to loss, and awareness of the disconnection that can come from unacknowledged, unexpressed pain. This was, after all, a part of each of their stories. If not a loss due to death, then it took another form: prolonged absence of a parent; prolonged absence from their parents due to illness (their own or parental); prolonged distancing from a parent due to grief or worry; separation from their world due to geographical relocation.

The unifying thread continued: each woman in the study described the pain she suffered from feeling isolated in her experience. None of them had a consistent figure present who accompanied them through the chaos that had come into their world. Each knew firsthand what it is to be lonely, bereft and disconnected from herself as well as from others. Each knew what it meant to throw herself back into busyness and/or high performance as a means of coping, even though her heart yearned for that "peace that passeth all understanding."

New Spirals

As the descent through suffering began to come full circle, the lives of the women in the study were affected by new twists and turns. At many of these junctures, they generously included me in their evolving stories. Unplanned by us consciously, our lives seemed deeply connected.

Over time, many of the co-researchers either referred similar women to me or invited me to share the research in settings which prompted other women's interest in analysis. Each brought her unique story, yet each seemed connected to the same familiar underlying archetype.

Of course, my intellect can argue that the population self-selects, which may distort a belief in the frequency of its occurrence. But the intuitive and instinctual aspect does not care. Something else seems more important than numbers: the inner experience expressed by those I have come to call World Weary Woman. I began to note that loss is not the end, but has the capacity to transform. In the hole suffering brings, an opening is made, not unlike a well. Such a place within World Weary Woman's psyche is nothing less than a birthing passageway: through death comes life anew.

I realized something else. Telling their stories in the confessional stage of analysis was only the first part of their redemption. By meeting in the oasis of a consulting room, a circle is circumscribed around a sacred rite of restoration. We need safe sanctuaries in which to explore our personal truth. But equally important is the educational aspect of the healing imagery, and its practical application through offering what we can of ourselves to our concrete world.

The process of developing our personality in such a way, as Jung reminds us, requires "insight, endurance and action."[5] These women are no strangers to action. Their challenge has been to trust the insights of their own feminine wisdom and endure what their circumstances and soul require. Reconnection is the key. But it must be a reconnection with what matters to our very depths. Sadly, like all of us, World Weary Ones can miscalculate. As one woman said: "My ladder is up against the wrong building. What happens in that structure and whether I measure up to their expectations mean less and less."

Using the Wrong Yardstick

What happens when we use the wrong measure? Very simply, modern woman, who suffers deeply in her soul, has been working to earn her "gold watch," so to speak, by living the conventional life, accepting that American institution of our fathers and grandfathers where one was rewarded with such a gift upon retirement after many years with a single employer. We, the World Weary Ones, are challenged to recognize when we are living the power way, and then ask ourselves whether we are willing to resign from participation in such races. The issue is not "doing," nor even the excessiveness behind the need to "do." Rather, the question posed is: "Whom does my doing serve?"

Anna, referred by her physician because of her chronic somatic complaints, brings an initial dream to her first analytic session with me. Four months earlier, this stately, five-foot-ten-inch African-American had become a widow. There is something about Anna which is compelling. Perhaps it is the fact that, despite her busyness, there is a certain look in her eyes, a certain light in the darkness, which suggests that "someone is home." I have the impression that her loss is far from the first and that she is a strong survivor—someone ready to dig into her own underground and willing to do the hard work this entails. She exudes a sense of intentionality without having hard edges. Though recently and profoundly wrenched, her depth of feeling is clear. A World Weary Woman in every sense of that term, she dreams the following, which includes the first image of her husband since his death:

> I am at work. It is night. The janitor is bringing in baskets and baskets of papers that someone else has handled. All the others have gone home.

---

[5] *Letters,* vol. 1, p. 375.

> They are with their families. I am completely alone. The faster I work, the more garbage baskets the custodian brings in, dumping the contents on my desk. Soon, there is a mountain of papers completely covering my desk. I look at my watch. It is getting later and later. I am hungry, really hungry. But if I don't finish the work, who will? and how will I get my raise and promotion? In the middle of this worry, my husband comes into the room. He stands at the doorway and looks at me smiling. He is radiant. Then he says to me: "You are neglecting what must not be neglected. Gold watches come in many forms." Then I awaken with a fast-beating heart. He is telling me something important. I am worrying about all the wrong things.

Fate leaves us lonely when success is all. Unfelt, unexpressed Eros leads to such a condition. Instead of following her own instincts honestly, this fifty-year-old woman has spent most of her life opting to do what impresses and pleases and makes others happy. She is too concerned with convention and appropriateness, which kills what is real inside her. Finally, the rage builds up inside Anna to such an extent that she erupts internally, the anger for self-neglect breaking into waking life through migraines, eczema, hypertension. In her case, if she can learn to retire from the need to be so industrious at the expense of her own soul, it is possible that she can connect with her true feelings, which can in turn lead her to who she is. This will be enough: that she serves what is real to her. She may no longer permit herself to stay too long in situations because she ought to. So, in lieu of this, we are left to relinquish our quest for the gold watch, to use our time well, working with what comes, whatever it is.

For some time I believed the essential issues for this particular type of woman to be loss and disconnection. My experience and theirs have helped me modify this perspective. The source of this disconnection is deeper than interpersonal, more ancient than strictly personal. When the archetype beneath World Weary Woman's high performance behavior is constellated, her loss complex is activated. That is to say, her reaction to her situation carries a highly charged emotional tone which seems irrational, excessive. However, when she can stay connected with the immediate thread of her experience, and not flee into trying to be reasonable, she fares better. Staying connected to that thread which reunites her body with her inner self brings healing imagery which can guide her in the direction of her own redemption.

What To Expect in This Book

What follows is a synthesis of what has evolved in my journey with World Weary Woman since conception of the project. Because contributors were at different developmental stages in their own personhood at the onset of the study, much of what was reported ten years ago was expressed in a more linear language. Initially, most had difficulty with the irrational aspect of their feminine wisdom and its mythopoetic nature. Often they spoke in impersonal clichés. Retrospectively this is not surprising, because with less firsthand experience they identified strongly with the industrious woman archetype, not with their feelings. When they were younger, Logos was most valued. However, over the last decade they noticed that living intellectually inhibits their capacity to live creatively, symbolically, personally. Without Eros, we are left with a heap of dried-out bones—no marrow, no juice, no feeling.

This is what World Weary Woman has suffered, leading her to a depleted, compressed existence, overly identified with an industry of the sort that robbed her life of richness. As one put it: "Living in my head leaves the rest of me dead." Her life has forced her to question her attachment to the intellect. A desire for self-discovery has prompted her to experiment with expressing herself in more symbolic ways.

Were this investigation to attempt to express World Weary Woman's experience in the linear language of her past, we would miss the color emerging from her as she discovers the authority of the feminine way. Whether she or you or I like it or not, the feminine way is the way of meandering. Nature circles, undulates, coaxes, waits and, sometimes, pushes her own rhythm and way of communicating. Yet the fact that this is Mother Nature's way does not make it any easier for World Weary Woman to adapt to it. When under stress, her impatient "get to the point!" attitude is constellated, and she fears anything remotely resembling letting go and speaking intimately.

I am aware of issues surrounding the disclosure of one's own story. I recall Marie Louise Von Franz and Helen Luke cautioning that a woman must learn discernment regarding the telling of her narrative. To say too much, with the wrong intention or in an inappropriate environment, to people with hardened hearts can cost one dearly. On the other hand, I am learning that part of my process as a World Weary Woman involves placing greater value on my womanhood and how "she" speaks through each of us. I am discovering, for example, that she is not interested in universal rules. She prefers to take each situation as it comes. In hindsight, this is not surprising. The feminine is, by nature, related. The issue is how to walk with a foot in both worlds, inner and outer.

This is a real concern to World Weary Woman. She is accustomed to the persona of her profession. She is familiar with censorship of all that is of a personal nature in what she does. What she finds difficult is to allow who she is to inform her work in inner and outer worlds. Her suffering brings her to this realization. Not only has she short-changed those with whom she has intimate relationships, she has also cheated herself of knowing her feminine nature in the most intimate way—through ongoing dialogue with her own soul.

The Intention and Archetypal Theme

The intention of this work is not to suggest a method or technique for World Weary Woman or those who interact with her. Nor is the intention to provide a formal Jungian analysis of the archetypal fairy tales, myths and legends used here to amplify the findings. Those readers interested in such a pursuit can find a host of work by others far more able than I to quench such a thirst. The intention is rather to offer what we have been discovering as it speaks from the ground of women's firsthand experiences as they pertain to the theme of transformation.

The archetypal theme, however, is another matter. Apparently there does exist, through no conscious intent of World Weary Woman, a unifying, collective pattern whose template is ageless. For example, I was reminded that the experience of living "above ground in the head" is a very different one from appreciating contact with embodied experience. Anna put it this way:

> I've come for Jungian work because even though I am bright enough to know what I should do, or even how my problem began, it is another thing to take action. It's as if something stops me and I stay still when I should move and move too fast when I should stay still. I don't know what or who this is in me. But whatever it is, this unknown "thing" interrupts me from living as creatively, spontaneously and joyfully as I'd like.

Anna and her World Weary sisters expressed dismay at being cut off from feeling fully alive. She cannot live as freely as her heart desires. Fortunately, analytical psychology brings a rich mythological context to the suffering of such so-called fathers' daughters. It is my hope that what follows will contribute to an understanding of the nature of such a wound and its redemption.

When Does a Story Involving Suffering Begin?

One of the most difficult decisions is knowing where to enter this particular story. Increasingly, as the issue of suffering enters my life, it opens up new dimensions. Each new round calls me to an edge of myself I have not previously known. Even though I may have jumped down into its hole before, I suspect and fear that this time will be different. What will be waiting in the dark? Will I make it back out intact?

To circumvent the fear, we might be tempted to stay above the story's depth, through a chronological retelling of events. But that would miss the point disastrously. Life is linear only on paper, not in experience. One circumstance is woven into the next. Threads overlap. We move back and forth between them as if they form a fabric which helps us connect above and below, thoughts and feelings, spirit with matter, conscious with unconscious, until a unique meaning is spun somehow from the raw material of our lives. But at the time of each event, we are incapable of knowing its ramifications. At best, we are left to speculate. At worst, speculation leads to predicting the future which separates us from the reality of now. And the reality is, when there is suffering, we are like the grape in the press. So, we begin in the present.

2
Who Is World Weary Woman?

It is my practice to keep field notes. One such entry was made after fifty-four-year-old Esther visited me to begin analysis:

> They come. They sit on edge of chair . . . weight pressed forward, wearing out upholstery on front edges first; their intensity so great, it wears the fabric of the carpet away beneath their anxious stance. Barely breathing. They pause infrequently. Too busy trying hard to never miss a thing, leaving no stone unturned. Hypervigilant in endless search—searching and searching and searching. When will it stop? All floodlights scanning for their fatal flaw. That one thing . . . that one perfect answer; that simple explanation which will, at last, redeem . . . let them rest. Take in, digest that promise of peace that eludes the clutch and grasp. Anything but casual, their quest has been relentless. Looking, ever looking, for the answer. So that then, finally weary of strong-arming themselves against the world, from a pain that comes from too deep and dark a well, they can at last, weary of the battle, sink into those Arms. Rest. Renewal. A place in which to contain what has been neglected for far too long.
>
> In a world intensely searching for THE TRAUMA, THE INCIDENT, THE PERFECT DIAGNOSIS AND FAIL-SAFE TREATMENT PLAN and METHOD, the world has forgotten that these Weary Ones are not the pathology they wear. We confuse the letter of the law with the spirit. Not surprising. In the effort to find solution, we forget these women are anything but problems-to-solve. They are experts, themselves, in this approach. In fact, they have made it a full-time job . . . to change, alter, cut away, suck-out, like liposuction, anything which seems imperfect, too human, too ordinary, too plain, too small.
>
> So here they sit, across from me. mirror, mirror on the wall. Part of them only too willing to take on another project. Yet another time willing to do whatever the outer world asks—willing to prove, prod, produce more competence, exude more charm. Willing to please, perform, just one more time.
>
> Meanwhile, outside, in waiting room, the Other one, their Woman Number Two, sits silently and invisibly. She knows how to wait. She knows how to hear again, the theory, the idea, the expert opinion and

terminal judgment of her as "case." She sighs, grown weary. She, the neglected one, fatigued by the other's penchant for perfection, is tired. Pure and simple exhaustion. Sinking back into the couch that holds world-weary aching bones and muscles, not to mention heart and lagging spirit, she sighs once more. This spiritual fibromyalgia runs deeper than any diagnostic code. Maybe this time. If only this once, the door would open for her turn, her movement, her chance, her place, her niche, her voice and mark.

If only there would be a place for her hands and feet, her belly and breasts, her backside to wiggle and shimmy, to rock and roll, to bump and grind, simply because it pleases her.

Woman. Sheer, unadulterated woman. Instincts. Good, reliable, instinctual nature gone dormant for too long. Not a blasphemy to God, but a Blessing of Creation. Absolved at last from a Sin that never was: the one of owning Her Original Innocence.

So, back to Ba. Back to Body. Back to Soul-food for her Soul. Body not as bad. Body as blessing. Body not as what to condemn, re-sculpt, redecorate, but body beautiful. Body not as endpoint, but body as container, for the depths to speak their sealed orders, so that when the Ferryman comes to say "IT'S TIME," we will not enter the boat from fear-of-life. Instead, we will dance on down to that tune too . . . no longer weary of the world, but renewed in having found the One within and lived it for all our worth.

Following this journal entry, I've been given endless opportunities to revisit the levels of torment that World Weary Woman feels as long as she is cut off from her natural dance. Like Esther, who looked increasingly to diagnosticians to explain her exhaustion, all to no avail. World Weary Woman's pattern is a knee-jerk reaction to outer expectations. This brings us to the necessity of defining a few basic terms.

Definitions

Type A behavior is defined by Friedman and Rosenman as

> an action-emotion complex which is exhibited by those individuals who are engaged in a chronic struggle to obtain an unlimited number of poorly defined things from their environment in the shortest period of time, and, if necessary, against the opposing efforts of other things, or persons in the same environment.[6]

---

[6] *Type A Behavior and Your Heart,* p. 67.

Such behavior is correlated with a high incidence of cardiac disease. Although this population is busy "doing," it is not a busyness rooted in instinctual wisdom. Type A behavior appears to be opposed to World Weary Woman's well-being. Perhaps the body is attempting to call her attention to the fact that she is in deep trouble. Cardiovascular disease is the leading cause of death for American women. The heart hurts in epidemic proportions.

This classic definition brings to light three important implications often overlooked in studies of Type A populations:

1) The first is that an axis exists for this behavior. Some individuals have been measured (Jenkins Activity Survey) to demonstrate high degrees of Type A behavior, others less.

2) Whatever the degree of their Type A behavior, these people are first human beings. Their nature expresses itself in many ways. When under particular stress, their characteristic response is to try to achieve certain ambitious goals. Yet there are times when their behavior is not affected by the activation of this complex. For the population in the present study, their complex-free periods seemed strongly correlated to a sense of safe, trustworthy connection with body and soul. Like each of us, World Weary Woman is a unique individual, with multiple aspects to her personality.

3) Under certain conditions, precipitated by different events, the Type A complex is activated. The question left unanswered by research has been: what underlying issue is associated with activation of the complex?

World Weary Woman is defined as an individual who exhibits a particular complex when she perceives a threat to something valued. When her loss complex is activated, World Weary Woman's habitual response is to attempt to achieve in a way that is excessive, leaving her disconnected from her feminine body wisdom and her creativity. Tired from such disconnection, she seeks a way of living creatively that allows her to express what awakens her heart.

I do not mean to imply that all Type A women are World Weary. The inferences drawn from this research come from the unique circumstances of each woman's shared story. Recall that each of the participants self-selected themselves. So they are seekers. It is this very soulful quest for further development of their personality that informs their progression.

World Weary Woman, then, by definition, is not content to live her life mechanically. The provisional life exhausts her and she knows it. She seeks a new tributary, a rivulet to quench her dryness, and is willing to detach from who she has been, despite her fear, in order to discover who she is meant to be.

My Original Encounter with World Weary Woman

Demographics

Four of the original eight participants were in the mid-to-late thirties (34, 36, 38, 39), three were in their forties (43, 45, 47), and one was in her mid-fifties (56). In terms of siblings, three came from homes where there was a younger sister; four an older brother or brothers; one was raised with an older male cousin (in addition to an older brother), and one had a male twin (as well as older brother). One participant was the middle daughter in a home of three girls. Thus, there was no consistent pattern of birth order.

Educationally, six of the eight had Master's degrees; two held Bachelor's degrees. All eight described a history of involvement in some form of personal growth experience which included reading, courses, and for some, seminars. Professionally, four of the participants led their own businesses, two of them in partnership. Of the remainder, two were psychotherapists, one was a business consultant, and one was in management and sales.

All eight women were involved in careers of service. Seven were married, one was divorced, three were separated from their husbands. Five participants were mothers. Two had two children each, three had an only child. The remaining three were childless. Geographically, three lived in the Northwest, two in the Southwest, two in the Northeast, and one in the Mid-Atlantic region of the United States. All were American citizens, as were their parents.

Each interview began with the following statement from me: "I am interested in your story. Specifically, I would like to know your perception of the major factors which most affected the way you developed during and since childhood."

Together we learned what these high performance women perceived to be the most important influences in their past, leading to their current status.

An Achievement Orientation

When a woman encounters great losses in life, whether her behavior is driven or not, it is understandable that she would search for a way to stop the pain, or protect herself from it in the future. Some strategies through which we learn to handle suffering continue to be productive; others become destructive to one's natural development. The latter is particularly so when the strategy is used to excess or inappropriately.

Type A women tend to cope through an achievement orientation. Ten years ago each of these World Weary Women presented themselves with a certain intensity, and some degree of resistance to relaxation. The intention seemed to be to reassure themselves of protection against both loss and disconnection from those they loved, as well as to ensure their visibility and connection in their own eyes—as well as those of others—warding off any threat to their mortality.

To achieve meant to succeed at something in a way that recognition and attention were gained. It did not appear to be related to the joy of the process. Achievement was equated with the final result rather than the process. It was interesting that achievement was related often to a strategy of caring for others. If they "care enough," as witnessed through the accumulation of achievements, perhaps then they would be protected from more loss and pain—as if building up a particular immunity. Here's how some of the participants described the need to achieve and how they organized their lives around it:

> *Jill, age 36:* I got a part-time job [in high school]. I arranged my schedule in my junior and senior years so I could get out early. I got acknowledgment from older people. That was very important to me. . . . I went through college quickly too. . . . I got much more satisfaction from working . . . because I felt acknowledged. . . . I hadn't had much experience in trusting peers my own age.

> *Claire, age 56:* It [working] was my way of getting acknowledgment . . . of getting recognition, and you know, being the only girl wasn't enough, and I was always feeling that I had to compete. . . . I did everything I was supposed to do. I worked so hard. I just went from 6 or 7 to 17.

> *Kate, age 32:* I'm supposed to be good, to be successful, real successful. . . . My grandmother would say: "Remember, you're a Sutherland!"—meaning you have the family name to uphold.

> *Freida, age 45:* When I had a job, I needed to have a big title. Probably my own sense of inner worth was lacking. Just who I am wouldn't be enough. My father couldn't brag about me then. . . . And then I wouldn't

be important. . . . So I'd think if I just worked harder and achieved more and more, then I'd be noticed.

Sarah, age 40: I was the one who was supposed to do it the way my father had. To succeed by doing it my own way despite the odds.

Conflict About Creativity

The interviews include many examples of a strong feeling tone that indicates an activated complex, in this case a creativity complex. While World Weary Woman relished being creative as a child, she turned her back on it in order to fulfill her ambition. Her creativity became distorted as she used it in service to whatever would please others. Rollo May's classic definition of creativity is "to bring something into being," something that did not exist before.[7] Linking creation and loss, May has indicated that under circumstances of significant loss in a child's life, in addition to suffering the loss, the child may also experience a disorientation that becomes problematic in itself.

Each of the women described a childhood in which she felt disoriented after being disconnected from what she valued. Yet before reaching adulthood, each was able to channel the anxiety from these losses and burdens into creative activities. These expressions became an important outlet. But the older she became, the more ambition took over. Too little space was left for her to explore creative living simply for the pure joy of it. If, for example, she longed to learn to sing or play the piano, she resisted unless she was assured that she would be successful, which was measured by whether an outer authority/audience responded positively. This is not surprising. Having and reaching goals was the major part of her identity. The structural tension between the world she wanted and the one she lived, albeit unconsciously, became redirected into her connectedness with herself and others in new ways.

Carey, then thirty-eight, put it this way:

> I would make up all the cheers. I was the designer. And I made up all the actions, and put all the actions with all the cheers. That was really creative for me. We didn't do gymnastics kinds of things, but I usually used my body a lot, like dancing. There was something really important about that. . . .
>
> And, then, just being with my friends, having relationships was an

---

[7] *The Power to Create,* p. 37.

art form. . . . I was always everybody's best friend.

Cooking was an art form. It made people happy. I could create, try things, experiment, and I was successful at it.

I was always trying to make the house look nice, but I never had anything to make it look nice. But that really didn't stop me. I just kept pulling together all kinds of things I could think of. I guess that's why I really appreciate aesthetics, beauty, harmony today. It takes a lot to pull it off. You have to be willing to experiment. I wish I could draw or paint. But I don't have the talent or means. . . . I don't necessarily see myself as being eligible to draw, but to create, and, I feel like I need to be guided, and yet I have this core that feels . . . so fulfilled by it.

Although few of the respondents were extraverted to the degree of Carey, each valued the importance of creativity. But almost every woman described herself as lacking in talent to make her creative images manifest in non-work-related ways (with the exception of a shared love of home interiors). When their work became noncreative, their enjoyment of it waned. The older World Weary Woman has become, the more she has grown accustomed to believing the following:

1) She is unqualified for creativity. She must have the right credential or training before she is entitled to step foot into the studio which speaks to her own creative voice.

2) She is creatively inadequate; her natural expression is not original.

3) She does not have the right to create as her heart wishes, thinking this too self-indulgent if it does not please others.

4) She is insignificant to Creation, the grand scheme of things, unneeded by the Creator for the advancement of life.

The Overall Pattern

Strategies Developed To Cope with Loss

The pattern that emerged was of a child who relished exploring her world creatively and with sensitivity. However, during her early years, she was confronted with the absence of a parental figure, which always included the father in some way. When this parent was not present in a way that was needed, a critical wound resulted. This produced the secondary wounds which caused inner pain and suffering, and often outer challenges.

To cope with what the outer world demanded at a time of inner suffering, the woman developed strategic behaviors which became protective. The difficulty ensued when the strategies became such that they cut her off from her body. The expression of her inner world became more difficult and costly. It estranged her from her own sense of authenticity and empowerment, and it disconnected her from intimacy with others when she desired it. Most important, she suffered from the loss of intimacy with herself. Over time, those parts of herself that were unused did not develop, comprising her unlived life.

In the original interviews, in World Weary Woman's perceptions of what had not been lived as she would have liked and what would be ideal to have within her life over the next ten years, four main categories were named. These included the desire to develop fuller relationships with 1) self-expression, 2) her body, 3) nature, and 4) other people, particularly significant others.

In light of these perceptions, it became apparent that when a young girl experiences a significant loss early in life, there are profound consequences. The predominant one for these women was that they found it difficult to trust. Worse yet, they lost trust in their own creative response to experience. During subsequent periods of chaos and loss, World Weary Woman broke connection with her own center of wisdom. She found it difficult to trust her own instinctual knowing at times when her world seemed to be falling apart.

When one is a child, and a parent disappears (be it through death, illness, work, neglect) the world may seem to crumble. Since such a critical hurt seemed to come at random, it is understandable that the child might want to "get it together," however she could. As Esther put it, "If you just try hard enough, it may not happen again. You just start juggling lots of balls, trying hard to keep them all going so no one gets hurt." Her need to maintain control, often through achievement, was an attempt to ward off endangerment through a strategy which promised insurance for her own viability. She hoped that she might have a future free of suffering.

Creative Incest

It was noteworthy that the women I interviewed described a sense of responsibility for the unlived creative life of a significant care provider. Often, this involved a desire to live the sort of creative life her father did not or could not. When he stopped living fruitfully, she assumed a certain responsibility for this task. As father's daughter, in many cases she began to identify with his dreams and expectations. None of the participants described her mother as "good enough"—one who does the best she can; accepting her mistakes as she goes, and course-correcting with forgiveness.

Instead, their portrait of mother was of a woman who suffocated with too much affection or not enough, and/or who doubted her own worth as a fully sexual, fully creative woman. Raised in such an atmosphere, daughters took on father's identity, which seems narcissistically wounded. Even where the daughter described her mother as nurturing, she seemed to assume the need to provide for her mother and family in ways that others did not. Psycho-spiritually, she assumed the role of parent. This was not correlated with birth order.

World Weary Woman's Reflections on Her Pain

At the time of the original study, World Weary Woman seemed to be completing a rotation of her development. She reflected on her perceptions of what factors in childhood led her to develop as she had. She indicated a loss of innocence in acknowledging and sharing the pain she had suffered. Her pain seemed to be twofold—the pain related to her sense of loss and neglect, and the pain that came from her industrious attempts to please others. She fancied an ideal scenario where she would know material success, and also feel connected in close relationships. All but two of the women in the study included figures of people in their idealized life drawings for the future.

World Weary Woman Now

Despite her efforts to insulate herself from loss, World Weary Woman's achievements proved false comfort. Although she tried valiantly to "beat the clock," she could not deter the inevitable turns of the life cycle. Her efforts to achieve did not give her immunity from loss, aging or suffering.

Over the last ten years, many challenges, some of which have involved profound loss, have come to each World Weary Woman in this study. She has ended and begun relationships. In the last decade the first eight participants in this research have experienced five divorces, one death of a husband, one death of a child, six deaths of parents, three remarriages and five births. Seven relocated, two of them twice. Seven have gone through major career shifts involving loss of a previous professional identity and the acquisition of a new one.

Four availed themselves of graduate or postgraduate education, which seemed to coincide with experiences of loss or disappointment in relationships (divorce, alcoholism of partner, disillusionment in partnerships, death, financial difficulty). Five suffered physical illness serious enough to merit hospitalization and surgery. Seven complained of weight gain. Five became menopausal. Each found herself "out in the world" in new ways, ranging from assuming or ending a motherhood role, assuming or ending a career role, assuming advocacy for a family member in distress: eating-disordered daughters (2), sexual identity difficulties (2), parental bouts with Alzheimer's (2), newly bereaved parents (2).

Each seems to be reconstructing her relationship with ambition, which became activated during times of pain in relationships. It is difficult for World Weary Woman to let go of relationships, even when painful. To do so seems to activate a deeper pain from which she distances herself. When she becomes caught in her ambition, she loses perspective, which further injures her relatedness to herself and her creations. It is hard for her to bring closure to what she values, for fear of the emptiness this might bring. She associates completion with pain.

Shifts and Realizations

There are hints of a new dawn for World Weary Woman. She appears to be seeking a deeper relatedness both internally and externally. Her need for ideal case scenarios for the future seems diminished. She speaks less of the future, more of the present, less about what she does, more about how she lives. There are hints of attitudinal shifts. She seems to be moving away from a certain innocence which needs to romanticize. She is reconsidering what her industry serves. As she reconnects with her body and its aging process, she notes the need for more space and meaningful creation. Her unredeemed losses seem connected with feelings of air-hunger, the need for "decompression" chambers—spaces where she can "breathe and learn to be myself—whoever that is."

Her antidote? The dawning realization that less is more. Small is good enough. Flaws create intimacy, rather than destroy it. She begins to reconnect with her own creative thread.

For the Original Eight, aging and a loss of some identity that was once very important, coupled with an increased need for self-awareness, brings about the necessity of an attitudinal shift. Such a shift seems particularly pressing when facing closures. The overidentification with ambition works less and less. Each expresses an increased need for self-awareness, albeit in different ways. The two youngest (now 42 and 46) indicate a desire for more will power, as wanting to "create the reality I want." For the remaining six (now ages 48, 49, 53, 55, 57 and 66), power is less the goal and method. There is now a greater focus on "accepting what I can't change, and changing what I can without so much confusion about which is which." Those who express a conscious awareness of the process they have undergone—most of whom have been involved in therapy or analysis—express a yearning for transformation that seems less ignited by ambition in the outer world. Their craving stems from a homesickness for what is within. Today, World Weary Woman's old way of being in the world, her need to be indispensable, leaves her unsatisfied. She seeks a simpler, less industrious reflection in the mirror. She describes wanting a "fuller relationship" with life, whatever this means, as she faces today and tomorrow.

Her situation may be thought of as similar to a story I heard about a man from the West who went on an expedition far away. For the first days, he and his guide and carriers traveled over many miles. Early one morning he arose and readied himself before dawn for another demanding day. But when he went out into the camp, no one stirred. Finally he awoke his guide and asked, "What is the problem?" To which his guide replied: "I am afraid I have very bad news. These people cannot move. They must first wait for their souls to catch up."

World Weary Woman needs her soul to catch up with her intellect. I once heard Margaret Mead observe that "education has made woman restless in her questing." It is this questing of the educated woman which can be the source of either her undoing or her true blossoming.

Unifying Thread in the Lives of World Weary Women

Each World Weary Woman, like everyone else, lives her unique story. My intention is not to diminish what differentiates her from others by implying that she can be put into yet another category or slapped with yet another diagnostic label. However, it is impressive that there is a unifying thread among the stories I have been privileged to hear. World Weary Woman seems to suffer a certain kind of wound, although the particulars of that suffering vary, as does the form of its redemption. Chapter Five will address the similarities of this wound.

World Weary Woman tends to be surprised and grateful to that that her plight is not as unique as she may have believed. When she discovers that she is not alone, that apparently her story is a part of an underlying pattern common to others, she finds relief from much self-inflicted blame. Heartened and renewed, she feels an urge to discover her uniqueness and calling.

What do I mean by this? As she discovers the limits of the life planned for her by ego alone, there is a gradual shift in attitude. She begins, in slow, tiny steps, to withdraw her attention from what drains, and moves toward a more creative way of living, transcending her previous identity. She outgrows what limits her well-being. Simply put, she experiences a change of heart. It is this change of heart that eases her burden and reconnects her to the joy and pain of living, loving, her own truth. This shift helps her find compassion for her ego that struggles with the demands of the world. Stewardship through creative devotion becomes essential. She does not abandon the world when she reclaims herself; rather, doing so assists her to serve with greater meaning and delight.

Possibilities and Cautions in the Analytic Process

Until such a change of heart occurs, World Weary Woman's industry serves personal ambition. What constellates her industry? Adept at hypervigilance, with a history of loss, she quickly scans the environment in which she finds herself. Esther, a fifty-four-year-old Jewish woman, imagines herself as if she were walking across a battlefield, wary of land mines. Anna calls this hypervigilance her "street smarts." World Weary Woman knows she must find a more peaceful way to move, but she presses on. Her instinctual knowing slips, unnoticed, into the background. All this happens so quickly that there is no palpable pause between instinctual wisdom and action. Too quickly filling the abyss between what she senses and what she does, the healing space is lost.

It is in this very imperceptible pause, if cultivated and nourished, that World Weary Woman's healing may reside. The analytic process can offer such moments during which to step from "doing" into "being." Such an immersion brings terror before redemption, for she must face the space she fears, yet needs.

Spending time with a World Weary Woman can be taxing. Given her developed ego that tends to overidentify with ambitious achievements, it is easy for analyst, friend or lover to fall into the trap she herself has set, yet also has been victimized by. The trap is the seduction into the part of her which invariably takes its turn first.

This part is compelling. Anything but boring, her life in the outer world can sound like a *Who's Who* article, crowded with social activities that seem meaningful to the extravert. Rich with adventure, even flamboyance, here is a woman who has "been there, done that." Ironically, she does not see this in herself. Well practiced in comparing herself to others, privately she underestimates her capacities.

Here the analyst must proceed with caution. Our own voyeurism, our own unconscious, unlived life, if sufficiently impoverished, may cause us to be so swept up, so fascinated by her story that, mesmerized, we fall into her Bermuda Triangle and are lost at sea. This would be a great disservice to her soul and to ours. Our task is to remember that she does not lack applause. As long as we provide it, she will feel compelled to deliver. As a father's daughter, what she fears is the empty theater, not the full one. So, as the saying goes, she "keeps on keeping on."

The impoverishment is subtle. She appears to enjoy the applause, yet yearns for something deeper—the silent touch. This is what she craves: to touch life and be touched by it in ways that do not bring pain. That much she knows. What she fears is that there is no other kind of experience available to her, or that she "deserves."

We who work with World Weary Woman do well to remember that behind her times of productivity, aloofness, harshness or coldness when she feels the futility of her own self-imposed deadlines, is hurt—deep hurt. Since she is hypersensitive to criticism, we must take great care not to attack, in even the tiniest way. We must remember that despite her animation, she is ever-scanning for cues of danger. When she feels scrutinized for flaws, her defenses activate. If we are uncomfortable expressing our own tender feelings, this tends to evoke the most alarm in her. When our hearts are closed to her, she will harden hers, judging imperfection in herself. She becomes hierarchical, which can result in a battle of will. She meets us on the ground we offer. Our test, as well as hers, might be to accept that we are meeting on common ground. The ground becomes more fertile when we relax our own defenses.

If she senses danger or pressure to do what she feels she cannot, we might notice a difference in the analytic interaction. When World Weary Woman feels judged or negatively scrutinized, the part of her psyche which feels demeaned and dismissed becomes activated, industrious. We may begin to wonder who is scrutinizing, and to what end.

The Antidote

In the process of World Weary Woman attempting to provide for her world, if she feels attacked by criticism, this brings up her own self-criticism, even if this is not apparent to those around her. In Jungian parlance, she falls victim to a negative animus attack. That is, her distorted masculine attitude turns against her. If she can note the intensity of her feeling and contain it, recognizing it as disproportionate to the actual situation, it will be a first step in learning to honor what she feels. This comes by refusal to dissipate what she feels, despite the disapproval of others. If she can do this, then the atmosphere is prepared for her to become a conduit of what she feels—now a creative urge rather than a destructive one. With creative intentionality, her feelings can find a resting place, in journal, paint, clay and so on—any touchstone through which she can express and embrace what reflects herself back in concrete form.

Fear of Being Unlovable

It is World Weary Woman's compensatory doing-ness that takes her into therapy. She has chosen to function in the outer world by producing what appears successful in the eyes of others. For her to acknowledge to herself that this coping strategy does not bring what her heart needs is an acceptance of failure. This is devastating to World Weary Woman, for she fears that without accomplishments she is unlovable. It is not surprising that, according to the literature, these individuals rarely seek psychotherapy. She is unaccustomed to accompaniment. To ask for it is to change an habitual way of being in the world. The challenge to us is no less than to her—to open our hearts to who we are and to who we are becoming in her presence. Do we ourselves dare to grow? Do we dare admit that we, like she, are not a "finished product," but rather, as we say in the studio, "a work in progress"?

Such daring in ourselves or those who come to us as World Weary People challenges American cultural norms in which doing—even excessive doing and achievement—are much approved and generally rewarded. But the issue is not simply World Weary Woman's "doing," nor even the excessiveness behind the need to do. Rather, the question posed is, "Who does the "doing" serve?"

Roots in the Past: A Developmental Picture

Overidentification with the Masculine

When World Weary Woman experienced loss in childhood, she lost her innocence as well. Such pain can force us into differing strategies of defense to ward off unendurable suffering. Each of the women in the study gravitated to a success strategy connected with the masculine principle.

They developed their rational powers and tended to use whatever behavior was most likely to preserve their sense of control. They developed and relied upon will power in both ordinary times and disastrous ones.

When they encountered difficulties, they learned to dismiss their wounds and needs with a "nothing but" attitude. Such an attitude demeans what Eugene Gendlin might term the "felt sense" of a profound experience such as loss.[8] In every interview this attitude surfaced in a form which diminished the emotional toll of the experience. Anna put it this way: "Of course it was hard when my father became ill and I lost him when I was seventeen. He worked hard all his life to support us, to earn his gold watch. But everyone has something tough in their life. Why did I have the right to feel sorry for myself? The responsible thing was just to go on."

Connecting with her feelings is often thought of in terms of irresponsibility, and, worse yet to World Weary Woman, self-pity. Instead, she has opted for whatever would bring fast results and ward off the necessity of feeling what she must if she were to pause and wait for her body to respond. We must not be led astray by her busyness. We must not forget that she is still searching for her own completion as she becomes more conscious. It is through her growth and development that she finds meaning, or as Jung called it, "individuation." It is this process of individuation by which every living thing becomes what it was destined to become from the beginning. Ten years ago, each participant conveyed a sense of having a destiny, although she may not have been able to identify it—as if there were a secret she was seeking and it sought her. Indeed, this secret buried in her core both precipitated and frustrated her creative expression.

Action as Compensation for Absence

World Weary Woman suffers from the assumption that action is invariably better than inaction, which she sees as slothfulness. So when it comes to suffering profound loss, the difficulty she experiences seems related to her excessive use of a busyness strategy which attempts to regain control, even though it is impossible. A huge part of her struggle pivots around an attitudinal shift with regard to what makes action useful and what makes it useless. Her lesson is one of discovering that busy activity which is unconnected to building intimacy with herself is the true idleness. If she is to redeem her suffering, she must learn how to meet her true self.

---

[8] See Gendlin, *Focusing*.

From learning to build a friendship between her ego and true self, she can then meet others.

We know that these women suffered parental absence long ago, in a number of forms. But there was also another kind of absence: the feeling of distance between their world as children and the world of grown-ups. Often this was the result of at least one parent's preoccupation with his or her own concerns, overlooking the needs of the child. An extreme example is that described by three women whose childhoods were marked by the death of a parent. During and after the deaths, they lived in homes that remained mute on the subject of bereavement. Other women described times of parental or sibling hospitalization when their fears went unnoticed, leaving them isolated. Still others described feelings of having been abandoned by their mothers, who in their need to please their husbands, neglected their daughters who then felt pushed to please in similar ways.

Nine years after Maria Theresa's initial interview, this small-boned brunette of Italian ancestry shares her experience:

> Since we spoke the first time about my growing up, I've thought so many times about the consequences of my dad's work taking him away so often, and about how I push myself too hard. I have always felt my dad was our hero, and my mom the villain, until a few years ago. I told myself that dad had to be away because he made the money. I rationalized his absence and stuffed my feelings into the closet. No wonder I've had a yo-yo weight problem. I stuff myself when I'm too afraid to feel the depth of what's real, especially when I feel cut off from relationships that mean a lot to me. Even though I'm 47 years old, when my partner or closest friend is preoccupied, I am reduced to a four-year-old little girl. It's like I fall into this zone where I'm mute. I'm trying to tell them that I need to be close, to be comforted and reassured that I'll be OK, but they seem not to notice either that I'm there, or that what I feel has any validity.
>
> This reminds me of a repeating dream I've had for years. I'm running after my daddy. He's getting into a taxi to go to the train station in Boston. His back is to me. Even though I call out to him, he doesn't seem to hear me. The cab leaves. I'm on the curb with my mother. A tear rolls down her face. She tells me to smile and wave, because Daddy likes us happy. I am outraged, but I do what she tells me. I smile and wave like a god-damned puppet.
>
> In reality, my memory is pretty blank about just what we did when my father was gone so much. We stayed busy. There seemed to be this endless list of chores to help my brothers and me keep occupied. Maybe the

chores were to push away the cold blue gray winter that went on and on and on. Even now, my body remembers that sensation. I HATE THE COLD to this day. I get cold whenever I'm not knowing exactly how to get the love I want that keeps slipping through my fingers.

I'm starting to realize two things through my analysis recently. My dad expressed more warmth than my mother, but my mother had no one there for her feelings, either, when he was physically or emotionally gone. I've been so busy blaming my mother for my father's absence that I failed to recognize my mother's pain. Where was she supposed to get intimacy? She must have felt invisible, too . . . like her role was to be the puppet wife who performed. She used to hum this song over and over that went: "Smile, though your heart is breaking . . ." We were both play-acting.

A Cost of Absence—Frustrated Archetypal Intent

During painful times in childhood, without an emotionally present parent, World Weary Women were left without a source of love and trust. In the language of Anthony Stevens, this can be said to frustrate archetypal intent.[9] Without a feminine presence of mothering that conveys a "good enough" atmosphere for development, how can the child learn to trust that all will be well? Without this foundation, these little girls learned that they were alone in the world, and they learned to compensate. They became responsible for themselves. They learned to protect themselves. Unfortunately, they hardened their hearts when support may have been available. What they did not master is how to receive. Frightened of vulnerability, they became masterful at staying busy to ward off pain. But what this also distanced them from was pleasure.

Not only D.W. Winnicott, John Bowlby and Melanie Klein knew the importance of what the former called a "good enough" mother. Jung, too, knew that a mother's continuous presence is essential if the mother archetype is to be activated *within* the child. Jung adds a crucial element, which is the feeling tone of the mother's atmosphere. It is this that catalyzes something profound within her child—the activation of the little one's inner mother, through which the child "reads" her relationship to the world. If the child's perception of the "mother out there" is distorted, so too is the child's capacity to cultivate her inner mother, which she will need if she is to grow and develop throughout her life. If our relationship

---

[9] See *Archetype: A Natural History of the Self.*

with our personal mother is problematic, this affects our capacity to nurture and nourish our feelings, instincts and relatedness to the world. Without healthy feeling mediation, a woman is left to the devices of a harsh animus with its impulsive actions, fast-paced judgments, "to-do" lists, and opinions which are global, conventional clichés, unrelated to the specifics of the present situation. Such a person is disenfranchised from her natural womanhood. This is World Weary Woman's plight.

Reactions to Midlife Losses

A Call to Course-Correct Ego One-Sidedness

A discussion of midlife losses experienced by World Weary Women does not suggest that they have a higher incidence of life changes than "non-weary" women. These women have endured the usual losses experienced by others of their age. What is noticeable, however, is their tendency to face profound losses with their characteristic industriousness.

Jung asked his students, "What is the dream trying to tell us?" Answering the question helped to course-correct ego one-sidedness. Similarly, we might ask World Weary Woman what her driven behavior is trying to tell us. Could it be her call to reconnect with her soul? Within the health care professions, it is well known that there is a self-regulating tendency at work in the body. When there is trouble in one system, the body does what it can to set things right.

Jung's work points to this reality at work in our psyche also. When we go adrift psychologically, emotionally, mentally or spiritually, a course-correcting mechanism goes to work. Paradoxically, the symptom is not only a messenger of trouble, as we learn in allopathic medicine. It is also a messenger conveying symbolic cure.

Within the literature on the Type A personality, the emphasis is upon symptoms as negative, something to be eradicated. Anger and anxiety are viewed as toxic rather than in terms of what they might be trying to communicate. Protocols have been developed which tell Type A people to learn to relax. Ironically, this very "prescription" (as previously mentioned in connection with Anna) tends to cause more distress in such a person. Each medical referral I have had over the last ten years of such an individual shares similar frustrations. When a physician tells her to "just calm down, take things easier," she feels annoyed. More than a few have told me that this brings up feelings of rage at themselves, for "something must be wrong with me that I can't do such a simple thing."

Historically, World Weary Woman answers her difficulties with attempts to be perfect, and perfectly good. She is not inclined to look for interior solutions until she encounters a form of suffering so profound that it stops her in her tracks, and her usual coping strategy does not work. She can no longer defend herself against her pain. It will not be quelled until she submits. There can come a time when World Weary Woman runs head-on into the realization that her will power will not only not solve her problems, but also that her head must give way to her soul. Her psyche leads her down into what lays embodied in her unexplored depths, however it manifests itself—through her dream or waking images, or physical symptoms. When her loss is profound enough, the pain reconnects her with that old, still-bleeding wound.

Desperate Measures, Finding New Ways

When this moment comes, and has her undivided attention, World Weary Woman is forced to face the fact that not only can she not control her suffering, but that it will persist in its present form until she enters its very nature, hears its message and responds to what is learned by attending to the creative task of living in a more authentic, soulful way. She must return to ordinary planet Earth. When her industrious attitude does not solve her problem any more than her intellectualizing does, she must acknowledge that and bare her scars.

When confronted with the unexpected, each World Weary Woman described a preference to "figure out the solution" and then to "get busy and into action." Without exception, such a strategy finally failed dismally. The head cannot solve, nor can it hold back forever, what is troubling the heart. What is in their soma carries such discomfort that in 33 out of 36 cases reported, the individual has sought professional counsel. This is noteworthy if we consider that previous literature has reported that Type A women have a very difficult time admitting their need for help. They ask for help only as a last resort. The very act of asking is an admission that the carefully constructed persona of self-sufficiency is crumbling. That admission can be as traumatic as the precipitating loss. It is a double-edged loss, a complicated grieving from wounding so deep that even the woman who suffers it doesn't know its full depths.

When assistance is requested, the woman must accommodate the violation to her self-perception as being able to "handle whatever must be handled" on her own. More than a few of these women reported initial feelings of embarrassment in seeking therapy, for to them it meant they had failed. But something of such urgency has broken through from the unconscious that they could no longer use their routine abilities to maintain a sense of control.

Pain forces us to face our blindness, our unconsciousness, and so becomes our rite of passage into the discovery of our own depths through acceptance of what the Fates have assigned us. Unless she does this, World Weary Woman appears to be living successfully, but she lives the power way, not the natural way; she can take action, but is not related in a feeling way.

Action is double-edged. There is useful action and useless action. World Weary Women come from a culture where industry is valued and inactivity is not. The collective Western judgment is that doing nothing is negative. This poses a problem for modern women, because the feminine principle is based on receiving. Mother Nature insists on receptivity to what comes. Childbirth is a good example. As the fetus moves through the birth canal, there are times the mother must push, and others when to do so would jeopardize the baby's healthy delivery. She must discern when to act by doing and when to act by being—that is, to receive what is in process without interference.

Invisible Wounds Prompt the Search for Alternative Paths

At the time of the original interviews, the women were at various stages of being "out on the highway." Over the following ten years, each has taken her turn in some sort of rest area. Each seeks a return to the compassionate ear and the contemplative mind—and through this, the restoration of meaning to her life. When "throwing myself into activities to keep myself busy so that I don't have to feel what I'm terrified to feel" fails to bring relief, World Weary Woman begins to reframe her relationship with suffering. When she can no longer run from it, it is this very experience that helps her find another way to relate.

Such a World Weary Woman has a dream. . . . In waking life Leah is a successful, well-educated forty-nine-year-old, with Scandinavian roots. She cares about how she presents herself to the world. She is responsible in her duties, both at home and at work. Since she entered midlife, she has noticed not only changes in her hormonal system, including the usual hot flashes, irregularities and dryness, but a certain type of fatigue that is deeper than simply being tired. Leah is experiencing soul fatigue. She notices that increasingly she has to push herself to do what she doesn't want to do, to appease those who demand her attention. Early in analysis she brings the following dream:

> I am in the waiting room outside the consulting room of my analyst. I look at my watch. The hour has grown very late. Another woman is in there. Her session is going late and spilling into my time. I am getting anxious. More time passes. I am now furious. She is using up my time. Finally she leaves. The therapist comes out and apologizes. I say nothing. There are only a few minutes left for me. As I sit down on the couch, I see the other woman has left behind her eyeglasses. The frames are made of tortoise shell.

What might this dream suggest? We find in Leah's dream three women: 1) herself, who as dream ego is not getting the attention she requires; 2) her therapist; and 3) an "other" woman. The masculine element is missing. Even though the hour of her life grows late, shadow sister steals this World Weary Woman's time. The therapist allows this, leaving the dreamer anxious and angry. Who is this Woman Number One within the dreamer, who in waking time usurps life? Might this be a commentary from the psyche that collusion is going on between analyst and this analysand who "talks too much"? On the objective level, this is a possibility. In what way has Woman Number One been monopolizing the dreamer's life? What is the dream message for the analyst? What "tortoise way" of seeing has been left behind?

When this dream was addressed in the analysis, the dreamer realized that she had fallen victim to her industriousness, not only in the outer world, but also in our analytic work. Like Anna and others we have met earlier, Leah's Woman Number One ambitiously strives to earn that metaphorical gold watch awarded by the collective. Her striving crowds out intimate contact with what is hidden, like Anna's dream of the janitor.[10] During her initial sessions, she brought figurative baskets of words, few of which conveyed anything that made real contact with what she felt. Frightened of intimacy, Leah's customary defense was to "keep the conversational ball rolling" with storytelling that left no space for soulful contact between ego and Self, much less between us.

---

[10] See above, pp. 21f.

Through the transference, I became more aware of her fear that, once again, the other Leah would be left outside the consulting room, not getting what she needed. It was painful for her to admit her feelings. To do so meant that she had to encounter her grandiosity in protecting the analyst as well as herself. Each of us had to discover a "tortoise way" of framing what was happening in the process. As it turned out, much of Leah's analytic work has pivoted around her conflict with the masculine "doing" attitude she holds, and the feminine "being" attitude, so long disregarded. The challenge for World Weary Woman is to find the inner analyst who can mediate between inner room and waiting room, inner world and outer world.

Leah and her World Weary Sisters are fearful of what they will find if they surrender their compensatory need for industry. They are frightened of being overwhelmed by inner urges, contents and demands. It is not unusual for World Weary Woman to fear a mental breakdown.

It should not be surprising that it comes as an enormous relief when World Weary Woman can reframe her imagery in terms of a spiritual crisis. Jung's model of the stages of life proves especially useful in understanding the challenges of aging. Jung reminds us:

> Man has two aims: the first is the natural aim, the begetting of children and the business of protecting the brood; to this belongs the acquisition of money and social position. When this aim has been reached an new phase begins: the cultural aim.[11]

> From the middle of life onward, only he remains vitally alive who is ready to *die with life.* For in the secret hour of life's midday, the parabola is reversed, death is born. The second half of life does not signify ascent, unfolding, increase, exuberance, but death, since the end is its goal. The negation of life's fulfilment is synonymous with the refusal to accept its ending. Both mean not wanting to live, and not wanting to live is identical with not wanting to die. Waxing and waning make one curve.[12]

Until World Weary Woman is ready to confront and accept her mortality, she races to beat the clock, as if she can outwit Fate itself. Unless she can accept life's end, she remains trapped in a race to satiate ego needs.

---

[11] *Two Essays on Analytical Psychology,* CW 7, par. 114. [CW refers throughout to *The Collected Works of C.G. Jung]*

[12] "The Soul and Death," *The Structure and Dynamics of the Psyche,* CW 8, par. 800.

Since the bulk of her time and ambition has centered here, her work has become a hungry god she has devoted all her energy to feeding. But this god lies dying, and she must find another.

Characteristics of World Weary Women

World Weary Women have strong, functioning egos. That is, their sense of "I-ness" is intact, despite acute sieges with confused direction and a paucity of meaning in what they do. Overall, they present a picture of women who are well adapted to the requirements of the outer world, with well-developed skills. Frequently they hold responsible positions of leadership and care-giving. Yet, based on this research, they are also likely to experience one or more of the following characteristics:

Increasing periods of excessive weariness
Symptoms of alexithymia[13]
A sense of unrelenting tasks
A sense that there is never enough time/resources for themselves
A sense of being last on one's own list
A sense of spiritual barrenness, despite outward appearances of okay-ness
A vague sense of inner discontent
A fear of betraying others if they take their duty to their own soul seriously
A history of having felt betrayed by competitive females
Impatience: "I don't have time for stories and doing what I want."
Difficulty in spontaneous, creative play
Gives approach-avoid, mixed messages: Invites closeness in response to her yearning for warmth and deeper connection, yet pushes away.
Fear of losing herself in intimate relationships

---

[13] "Psychiatric lexicons contain the term alexithymia for the condition of certain people who cannot describe or recognize emotions, who are able to define them only in terms of somatic sensastions or of behavioral reaction rather than relating them to accompanying thoughts. Such people are handicapped by their inability to understand what feelings are." (Jeffrey M. Masson and Susan McCarthy, *When Elephants Weep: The Emotional Lives of Animals,* p. 10)

3
Natural Womanhood

Toni Wolff's Model

What is the archetypal nature of womanhood from which World Weary Woman has been severed? What can be said of the cross-cultural patterns of a woman's nature, whose ancient roots still inform us?

Jungian analyst Toni Wolff proposed just such a model, based on the premise that each woman expresses one dominant aspect of the feminine. There are four types, a quaternity of womanhood. The axes are derived from one polarity which is impersonally related (Amazon—Medial Woman), and the other which is personally related (Mother—Hetaira). Wolff writes:

> They might be referred to as the psychic forms of the Amazon, the Mother, the Medial Woman and the Hetaira. As a rule, one form is the predominant one, and may be joined by another, while the third and fourth are at first unconscious and can be made conscious and integrated only with difficulty, and during the later part of life. In view of the fact that all four forms can be traced back in the history of culture, they are probably of an archetypal nature.[14]

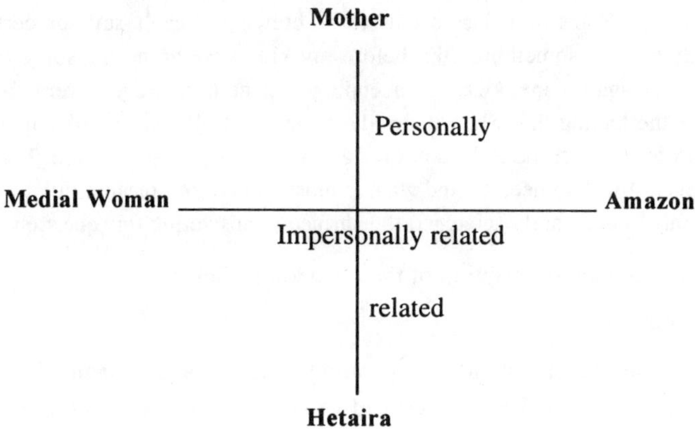

[14] "Structural Forms of the Feminine Psyche," p. 5.

The notion of preexisting structural forms is not new. Before the close of the nineteenth century, a German anthropologist by the name of Bastion referred to them as "elementary ideas" which shape humankind's reality. In the twentieth century, Jung examined empirically the interplay of archetypes and typology in the expression of personality. An adaptation of his work to the feminine psyche followed, created by Toni Wolff and others. Some years later, the quantum physicist David Bohm referred to this living reality which shapes our reality as the "implicate order."[15] Apparently, there is a morphogenetic field that surrounds and shapes consciousness, which includes human personality.

This is not an easy influence for World Weary Woman to grasp. She is accustomed to looking for answers which are rational, causal and matter-based. But when she reflects on her own development, she refers less to the importance of will power and logic, and more to the mysterious forces shaping who and how she is in the world. She seems to be making room for the "other" that is operating within. She is, as Maria Theresa put it, "having her say." In her words:

> I guess you could say I am a feminist. My mother was one, and my mother's mother, too. But that only gets me part of what I want. I call this my "soldier." My soldier helps me marshal my strength and resources to become independent. I am proud of what I've accomplished. But there is another piece of me that is bored to death with marching on all the battlefields, slaying dragons one after the other. Even soldiers need rest. Something else seems to be brewing. I can't say for certain what it is . . . something like before my kids were born . . . something nudging against me, kicking, hiccuping . . . getting bigger every day. I have the feeling that when it decides to show itself, we are all going to be in for some surprises! I don't need to prove I'm equal anymore. That is a given. But I do need to find what is most natural and meaningful to me. So far, I have barely scratched the surface in answering this question.

That is a good description of the Amazon archetype.

The Amazon

What is the archetypal intent operating within the Amazon, the natural expression of who she was destined to become from the beginning? Ac-

---

[15] See David F. Peat, *Infinite Potential: The Life and Times of David Bohm,* pp. 2f., 256ff.

cording to Wolff, the woman who functions in the Amazon mode has a penchant for partnership. She sees herself as equal to men, and bases her relationships on intellectual, masculine concerns and Logos. It is not uncommon for the Amazon woman to express herself in a gifted way which the patriarchal world understands well: a focus on achievement, making her mark. Since equality is a given in her relationships with men, her ambition can intimidate others. She feels comfortable on the masculine playing fields, and is energized by competition; she willingly asserts herself. The shadow of the Amazon is that she can be overly critical in relationships, corresponding to an overly critical inner attitude toward herself.

Maria Theresa's self-portrait suggests this tendency:

> Since our last interview, I've realized that for most of my adult life I've been most comfortable with men. Being open with women, especially if they are aloof or cold, makes me gun-shy. Men seem to get to the point better than women. They aren't as emotional or petty. They stay focused in ways women often don't, and they don't gossip in the hurtful ways women can. A man's testosterone is "on the table." The cards are laid out where you can see them. But with women, you never know. Often with women, what you see is different from what you get behind your back. It is only in the last few years that I've begun to open up; but it is with women who are safer, softer, not competitive. I'm used to the tougher ones in business.
>
> I'm thinking of a typical scenario. This woman, whom I'll call Liza, came to me with a proposal to partner a business. The idea came from Liza, not me. I was excited and saw the potential. "Potential" is my drug of choice. It seduces me into all sorts of things. Anyway, I agreed to work with Liza on the venture. For nearly four years I made sacrifices to build a solid business foundation, even though I felt like I was expected to sacrifice while Liza increasingly seemed to think she could coast along on my efforts. She was getting, while I was giving. I became resentful. When confronted with how she was sabotaging what was being accomplished, she denied the whole thing. What bugged me the most was that she never seemed to notice the sacrifices I was making. Ironically, she told me she didn't feel appreciated! That is precisely how I felt: unappreciated and unthanked. Is this what sisters go through? Neither of us have any. The whole thing became so painful to me that I offered my role to a man who was interested in working with Liza. I was angry, sad and relieved. Looking back on it, I can see over the past few years, that Liza and I have something powerful in common: each of us felt criticized for

not being "good enough" by the other. In my own analysis, I have begun to realize that I projected onto Liza the criticism I felt. I'm not saying she was entirely blameless; but I realize that I can be overly critical of myself and then assume criticism is coming from somewhere "out there." Sometimes I get too aggressive. Maybe it's easier to fight the Liza outside myself than to have it out with the Liza within. This is the peace talk I need most.

My most recent discovery is very scary. I have begun to notice that my competitiveness is, in part, a defense. Not all the time, because it's a useful skill when needed. But there are other times when it becomes a wedge between myself and people I care about. Like Liza, for example. I can obsess on how she has overlooked my needs. I can go around and around in my own mind justifying myself. My mother called this "licking your own wounds." I'm good at this. But below this is the thing that frightens me. Underneath my resentment and self-justification and martyrdom is my sadness. The pool of sadness is so deep that I don't want to touch it. Yet I know I must if I really want to find out who I am. There are layers and layers of disappointment that scare me. Maybe this is the real issue with Liza: my sadness at the lost opportunity to make contact. I want more closeness, yet fear it. Maybe this is why it's been easier for me to function in a man's world. Over there you get penalized for anything but a competitive spirit. A man's world is a risk-free zone for me. I can joke and strut around like a peacock, like the best of them, and never have to risk being vulnerable as a human being, in the female sense. But that is also my sadness. I've chosen a playing field which leaves who I am as a woman waiting in the bleachers. Maybe a better metaphor is that my softer side is "benched."

World Weary Woman's Amazon behavior is at least partly adaptive. Although Wolff suggests that a woman expresses her personality through one predominant structural form, my experience with World Weary Woman is that the expression of her Amazon archetype is cyclical. Women like Maria Theresa express their Amazon most when they sense they are nearing the jungle. She can sniff it out in a heartbeat. She reacts to perceived threats by mobilizing her strength to fight. As Maria Theresa implies, however, her feeling nature takes flight in the meantime. The typical response of World Weary Woman to stress is not fight or flight, but fight *and* flight. It appears that the Amazon archetype is activated at times when she requires a sense of fierce independence to feel safe. The Amazon within offers her a touchstone—a fortress from which she can defend her rights and needs, a place from which she can strategize to protect her territory when war seems imminent. And when the white flag is waved, she can step out from behind her defense camp to reveal who she is in other ways. Meanwhile, as she experiences new aspects of her nature which round out her personality, the inner Amazon base camp stands ready in the jungle—ready to receive her when she returns with more of herself.

This is what differentiates World Weary Woman from the classic Type A. The Type A personality chooses to remain in the competitive mode, with all the attendant consequences to well-being that are related to a state of high hostility. A case in point comes from a recent consultation with a classic Type A woman who completed her medical residency. Numb to her exhaustion, but troubled by her stress, fifty-three-year-old Margaret, a second generation Chinese-American insisted: "But don't you see? I can't take time to take care of what you call my inner life right now! I *must* get my business expanded, more profitable, before I rest! Everything else will just have to wait." Three weeks later she phoned me for another consultation. "My back has flared up and it's too painful to do anything. Help me get back to work."

In contrast, World Weary Woman chooses to develop a more full-spectrum response. For some reason, she feels propelled toward individuation. Her fate is that of the seeker. As Maria Theresa put it: "I have no other choice. I simply *must* find who I really am, even if it is painful."

With each progression World Weary Woman achieves in the growth of personality, she discovers a fuller range of motion. Inch by inch, her expanded personality frees her to play not only with her Amazon nature, but with the other structural forms of the feminine psyche that Tony Wolff described.

Since this cyclical nature differs somewhat from Wolff's model, let us return to her own words. Writing in the 1950s, Wolff observed that "the insecurity of many a modern woman regarding her own self and the essence of the Feminine" is found most where the feminine principle has been devalued to the point of disappearance.[16] Denial of the feminine is tantamount to disappearance of the soul. When we split off from our soul, we devalue psyche, whose "inner life . . . is the basis of individuality . . . . that organ for the experience of God."[17] Psychologically, what vanishes

---

[16] "Structural Forms of the Feminine Psyche," p. 2.

[17] Ibid., p. 3.

from consciousness is not eliminated. So, even though we may have severed ourselves from "the basis of individuality," that "organ for the experience of God" is building its strength in the unconscious until its need for recognition cannot be denied. What we ignore redirects itself into the world of the unconscious, where it festers and builds momentum until it forces itself over the threshold into consciousness. Without this self-regulating tendency of the psyche, we could find neither our own full personhood nor our experience of God, for the two are intimately related. Whatever it is in our nature that we've denied conscious expression comes back with a vengeance to create our greater wholeness.

The feminine principle is no exception. Not only do we seek reconciliation with parts of ourselves which have been split off, but the Self, regulating center of the psyche, also seeks integration with the ego.

The representation of feminine structural forms of the psyche offers a useful reference point for the struggle of World Weary Woman. Her persona in stress-riddled environments is as the Amazon. However, nature abhors imbalance and has a tendency to compensate one-sidedness. This is a consistent theme in the evolving story of World Weary Woman. From interviews and consultations, one fact is clear. World Weary Woman has a proclivity for movement. Given enough tension, as she has grown fixed and rigid, her psyche does what it must to ensure fluidity again. This brings an attitudinal shift from dominating ambition to increasing intimacy. Historically, ambition has been her prime motivation. But over the years, a yearning for intimacy is something she feels with increasing urgency. Fifty-three-year-old Marty: "I have my things. As a financial planner, I've made sure of that! But now I realize how much I need a life."

This trajectory is neither direct nor quick. Her psycho-spiritual shift is circular. Although she longs for intimacy, she does not get to it directly. She must learn to take her time, to cultivate it little by little. She learns that there is validity in the meandering way that is characteristic of the feminine, albeit suspect to her inner Amazon, who wants results, and wants them yesterday.

The Mother

World Weary Woman struggles to extricate herself from that aspect of her Amazon that barrages her with poisoned spears of self-criticism. She yearns to honor and learn to trust her instincts.

Often she has confessed to me: "I'm only just realizing how deadened

I've become. I don't think I even know anymore what or where my instincts are." I've heard something akin to this from women ranging in age from seventeen to eighty-three.

World Weary Woman learns best to locate and trust her instinctual body wisdom when she is in the archetypal field of Mother. World Weary Woman longs to feel safe. She fears that the tranquillity she seeks will never be hers. Wherever World Weary Woman feels safety and accompaniment, she is with the archetypal Mother. Whenever she is taken seriously, she is in the presence of Mother, an atmosphere which quiets and soothes her Amazon, so tired from being on twenty-four-hour duty.

As her Amazon realizes its right to rest, like the rest of her interior tribe, other members emerge. Alongside the emotional warmth of such a mothering source, these women feel heard, cherished, nourished. What I am calling the atmospheric presence of the Mother archetype, Wolff refers to as the "structural form of Mother." For me, structural form suggests a static state, whereas atmospheric presence connotes a certain dynamism which evokes movement, development. The archetypal intent behind Mother is progression of its young. A cherishing mother bears witness to our growth and supports our uniqueness.

Wolff describes the structural form of Mother as

> . . . cherishing and nursing, helping, charitable, teaching. Her instinct reacts to all that in man is in the process of becoming, or which is undeveloped, in need of protection, in danger, or must be tended, cared for and assisted. Without condescension it supports and consolidates what is unaccomplished and in need of help, and provides room for psychic development and greater security. The mother finds her fulfillment in her relationship to that which needs protection, help and development by endeavoring to strengthen it, so that in the normal case it can be dismissed from her care or, if this is not possible, it can be granted maximum security.[18]

World Weary Woman's Amazon aspect can relax most in the atmospheric presence of Mother, regardless of whether this archetype is evoked in the form of best friend, analyst or her own child. Whenever she feels warmth, she is at Mother's hearth. There she may warm herself more freely. She trusts that she is "good enough," and feels free to let go. As a

---

[18] Ibid., p. 6.

fifty-seven-year-old ex-nun put it:

> When I was away, I felt so uprooted from something that happens when I am here. It's an odd sort of disorientation or disconnection. But when you're here, I am like the Prodigal Son, or, I guess you'd say, the "Prodigal Daughter." I've come home. I know I am welcome here. I don't have to pretend I am not lost. I am lost, so I am found.

We who have been out in the cold need to find refuge in a place which warms what's grown numb. We need this experience in the outer world, so we can locate our own mother's hearth in our inner world. We World Weary Women want, more than anything, to come home.

Mother's Shadow Side

Perhaps part of our ambivalence in coming home is that we have experienced Mother's darker side. I am speaking here not so much of personal mother, although she has her shadow, too, but of the Mother archetype. Wherever we sense the development of new life being threatened, the negative aspect of Mother might be at work. This is that deeply disturbing "Mother doesn't want me to be born" reverberation which is so vague that it is easily dismissed. But when it flares up for World Weary Woman, it does so, as Anna says, "with white heat," often through body sensation. Mother means matrix, the primal ground from which we grow. The Mother archetype lives and speaks from there.

Increasingly, I see the darker aspect of the Mother archetype threatening the bodies of women referred by their gynecologists, family practice physicians and midwives. Perhaps because I was a nurse practitioner before I became a psychologist and analyst, I am more likely to receive such referrals. The signs of the negative Mother archetype at work vary: difficult menstrual cycles and painful menses, infertility, fibroids, painful intercourse, miscarriage, and uterine, ovarian and breast cancer, as well as other forms of cancer. Although each person's full story is unique, we do find a common theme in these cases: Mother, that is, matter/*mater,* has become destroyer. Her capacity to create physically has taken a harmful turn.

Sandra is a thirty-five-year-old Episcopalian priest who was referred by her physician. This meticulously coifed and dressed, slim and attractive blue-eyed brunette, came because she was having difficulties with chronic menstrual cramps and infertility, unrelieved by pain medication and medical intervention. She described a history of cramps,

. . . from my first period at age thirteen. From the very beginning, I hated having my period. I could see why my mother called it "the curse," just like my grandmother. My mother suffered with cramps until she finally had a hysterectomy at age forty-one. Both of us thought that part of being female was for the birds.

At twenty-one, Sandra had an abortion,

. . . which I had to do because my father and mother would have killed me if they'd found out, and I didn't finish college. I'm not sure which sin would have been considered worse, dropping out of school, getting pregnant, or being sexual. Alan and I knew the only sensible thing to do was to terminate the pregnancy. As a minister's daughter, another option would have been cause for ex-communication. You don't have to be Catholic in my family to be ex-communicated! Anyway, Alan was the only man I ever loved. But something happened after that period in our relationship which killed something. It was the only time in my life I felt passion and loved sex too. After that, with the few times I was in a relationship, nothing really worked. I don't know whether it was tension or fear I'd get pregnant, but intercourse began to hurt, the penetration. Intellectually, I can figure it out. But what I cannot do is figure out why it is that my husband and I can't get it together. I love David. He is a good man. I chose him in part because he'd make a great dad. He loves kids. He's busy most of the time counting the hours until he takes early retirement at thirty-nine from Microsoft. We have our big house and too many cars. We have the toys. But I can't get through the gnawing feeling that what is missing has to do with some sort of contact with each other below the head. David's dad is dead. His mother is constantly on the phone with him giving him advice, asked for or not. He says he feels like he is suffocating. She intrudes all the time, almost like she's jealous we want to have our own life. The funny thing is that although on the surface, she looks so different from my mother, underneath she is very similar. Neither of them can stand it if we want to get to some real level of communication. They are even more uptight than us.

The night before her session, Sandra had the following dream:

David and I were in the forest. I was handed a newborn baby, which I held closely. Suddenly, I felt danger and cried out to David. The sky was pitch black. Behind where I stood, two huge mother bears were coming my way. For some reason, they were furious and coming after my baby and me. We were running and there were huge rocks all around, and a river up

> ahead, because I could hear it. I hollered for help. We needed a boat to get away. I saw a woman there who I didn't know, but who looked a lot like you, blond hair and light eyes. I cried out to her for help and she smiled and said, "Relax." She motioned her hand toward the river and a boat that she had ready and waiting for us to get free. I awoke with a fast-beating heart, but with hope.

Archetypally, we are given an interior view of Sandra's psyche. She is entering the unconscious (forest at night), and given the opportunity for new life (the baby). Accompanied by masculine discernment (David), she realizes they are endangered. The dark Mother (bears of Artemis) has turned dangerous and menacing. But through her cry for help (dream ego's acknowledgment that it must submit to the higher authority of the Self), a shadow sister (blond, light-eyed woman) arrives with the saving thing—the boat (alchemical vessel, ego container) that can carry the endangered new life back to natural relationship with the dreamer's river of life. The dreamer's cry for help (supplication to the transcendent) shifts the direction of libido/life force and there is the suggestion of hopeful resolution by this action. The negative side of the Mother is counteracted through the dream ego's cry for help and the psyche responds by sending the nurturing aspect of Mother.

Nature abhors imbalance. Not atypical of an activated Mother archetype in a woman, Sandra marries a man she believes will make a good parent. She is speaking about David as father to her children. But unconsciously, she is seeking someone who can affectionately parent her own undiscovered nature. Whereas the Amazon archetype prefers an unconscious business partnership set-up, based on equality, the Mother archetype's intent is to select whatever partner will protect and ensure the development of her young. Not only does this apply to her children, but to the care and tending of her own inner children. The shadow aspect of this propensity is that if her mate wishes to develop in a direction which does not serve her perceived needs for her young, or the newly developed aspect of her own nature, she may sabotage his individual yearnings in order to serve the whole. This carries an interpersonal price tag.

Getting Help with the Bears

As World Weary Woman realizes that the bears are coming, she calls out for help. This is a major leap of faith. This is not the norm for Type A people. Prior to this time, she feels compelled to make it on her own, through her metaphorical dark forest, or as Sandra put it, to "tough it out on my own if I don't want to be excommunicated." Historically, she has had little practice in asking for help. The fact that she comes for assistance through analysis is a very hopeful sign. If it is meant to be, she will find a boat to carry her, not away from life but toward it.

Movement along this river requires not only that she disengage from negative Mother's inclination to attack and strangle her move toward personal autonomy, but learn to receive tender kindness with less suspicion.

World Weary Woman needs this contact with the life-preserving aspect of the Mother archetype. The importance of this stage in her relationships should not be underestimated. Those analysts, clergy, helping professionals, mates or family members who are fortunate enough to accompany her journey might miss this vital point, for her persona of competence can fool us. My experience is that underneath World Weary Woman's mantle of achievement hides a little one who hopes someone will notice, at last, that at times she trembles, doubts, fears and dares to hope, just like the rest of us. Do not be duped. The World Weary Ones in your life want tender warmth as much as anyone. This takes place in a nonsmothering, nurturing atmosphere. You need not be female to cultivate its qualities. It takes time, consistency and patience in extending yourself again and again, in the face of what appears to be rejection, before she can let go her fear and learn to trust that your helping hand is not a bear's claw in disguise.

If you can find the requisite patience, you may witness movement, too, which is nothing short of amazing grace. However, this does not come without an effort on her part to learn the importance of receiving, as she experiences her episodes with her "bear chase."

Psycho-spiritually, the developmental progression of her personality requires new musculature. Sandra expresses it like this: "I'm in a cool-down mode with my career muscles, and a warm-up mode with my own mothering muscles." She has put her finger on the pulse of World Weary Woman's need.

Not atypically, Sandra came to her first pregnancy with misgivings shared by others. This went beyond the standard, garden variety, new mother anxieties. When Sandra first learned she was pregnant, she became intensely anxious. She recalls feeling torn by doubt, especially as the pregnancy related to the fear that her career might be jeopardized:

> I know I should be happy, but I am depressed. What's wrong with me?

> I'm embarrassed to tell anyone how I feel, even David. It's not only that I know I'm ignorant when it comes to mothering, with the exception that I don't want to repeat my mother's mistakes. Maybe I'm afraid that when I have kids, I'll just go poof—vanish, never to be heard from again. What will happen to all the ground I've gained? I'm going back to work as soon as I can.

Not only is this sentiment conveyed by Sandra in her mid-thirties, but older World Weary Women have admitted their early ambivalence about birthing and child rearing. More than half the women who shared their stories with me described complications or challenges around pregnancy, and/or labor and delivery. Still others struggled secretly with serious private reservations about whether they would be good mothers—an issue of deep shame for them.

As an aside, I have noted over the past ten years, with great concern, an increasing number of teenagers and women in their twenties who express similar feelings. Living in a world which has increased the stress on women in the workplace, this may not be surprising, but warrants future investigation. We seem to have a growing population of World Weary Youth who long for deeper contact with the benevolent aspect of their own internal Mother.

Take Sandra's story. Much of her analysis, during pregnancy and postpartum care, focused upon basic reassurance that she would do no harm to her daughter, even though she was fearful. Initially, at times of greatest upset, she reverted to Amazon behavior as she stalked her how-to-parent books and tried to do what the experts said. But as she recognized this old pattern she was able to put it aside, bit by bit, and listen more closely to her own instincts. For her Amazon to come off duty, sometimes she required an extra hour of analysis. As she grew proud of increasing her willingness to fumble and be okay with it, she began to notice the special rhythm, language and personality of her little girl. As she relaxed into the hands of Great Mother, her own relatedness to mothering grew. This is what Sandra refers to as the "warm-up mode of mothering muscles."

The Medial Woman

As the warming progresses, World Weary Woman can find herself beginning to warm up to another part of her psyche, her symbol-forming function. Previously dismissing irrational realms as impractical, she begins to see the value in cultivating her interior life, which speaks symbolically. She rotates her focus toward what Wolff termed the Medial Woman. In a way, this makes sense. As she discovers that her Amazon can take a nap from its exhausting duties, and if she finds that something nurturing happens in her significant outer relationships, she finds increasing respect for her body wisdom—aware that her physical signs and symptoms, her dreams and synchronicities, and perhaps even doodles, are more than mere happenstance. When she heeds and acts upon the hieroglyphs her soul is sending—messages of guidance which no one could have predicted—her attitude takes a dramatic shift. Until then, she continues her "nothing but" attitude toward inner prompting, pretending it means nothing.

Maria Theresa's story provides an example. When she first came to analysis, she complained that she never had dreams or remembered them. It took eighteen months for her to bring the first dream she could recall. When it came, she described it as insignificant—an ordinary dream:

> I saw a dog lying half-dead in the road. Some witch-type woman was trying to run over the dog with her tractor, and threw it down a water hole or very old well. I was watching it from a great distance and could hear the dog whimper. I knew I had to help the dog.

When I asked Maria Theresa about her response, she said:

> You tell me. You're the doctor. I have no idea what it means. Anyhow, I don't have a dog and never did. They are too much trouble and they shed. I'm too busy with my work to have an animal. That would tie me down.

It took another year for Maria Theresa to return to her inner dog, which did not happen until she suffered such intense back pain that she was hospitalized. During two months of traction, her dream came back in a very personal dog. She began to appreciate how her psyche was trying to warn her about her interior witch, who was trying to run over her dog (instinctual relatedness to the needs of her body and soul) with overly ambitious career goals. This was a major turning point in her individuation process. Since then, when she has bouts of back pain, she explores the situation, as if she were living the dream, in order to identify in practical ways what action she needs to take in support of her own well-being.

It is Maria Theresa's growing relatedness to her Medial Woman, via deepening contact with the Mother archetype, which has made this possible. What are Medial Woman's "muscles?" Toni Wolff had this to say:

> The medial woman is immersed in the psychic atmosphere of her environment and the spirit of her period, but above all in the collective (impersonal) unconscious. The unconscious, once it is constellated and can become conscious, exerts an effect. The medial woman is overcome by this effect, She is absorbed and moulded by it. . . . She must . . . express or act what "is in the air," what the environment cannot or will not admit, but what is nevertheless a part of it. . . . The overwhelming force of the collective unconscious sweeps through the ego of the medial woman and weakens it, while on the other hand, the ego of the Amazon is strong, just because she keeps herself out of this abysmal background. By its nature the collective unconscious is not limited to the person concerned— further reason why the medial woman identifies herself and others with archetypal contents. But to deal with the collective unconscious demands a solid ego consciousness and an adequate adaptation to reality.[19]

Perhaps because World Weary Woman has developed her interior Amazon so well, she comes to her Medial Woman aspect via the Mother archetype with a sense of excitement and adventure. The fact that she has a symbol-forming function which connects her with the mysteries is sometimes terrifying. But discovering a deeper dimension of herself that has its own goal becomes compelling. When her connection to the personal and collective unconscious awakens through its symbol-forming function, she finds herself coming back to life.

One place I witness World Weary Woman's return to life is through our shared studio time. I teach "Painting from the Unconscious"—an experience of jump-starting the creative life. Since these women's lives have been spent in practical reality, they are not prepared for what they unearth when they engage in that psycho-spiritual dig of the creative imagination. They find the symbolic voice of the psyche stunning, and understand that their own dreams, fantasies and physical sensations have a unique wisdom.

The more World Weary Woman takes herself seriously, however, the more she realizes that her boredom and restlessness come when she bobs along the surface, rather than entering her depths. As she begins to honor her Medial Woman, she finds it is the depths of her soul which make it possible for her to return to everyday chores with a greater sense of vitality. As she counts her change at the grocery store or pumps gas for her car,

---

[19] Ibid., p. 12.

these experiences bring her back from the well of creative imagination in such a way that her relationship to these tasks becomes more intimate. She is a part of the web of life and it is a part of her.

This is an important realization. One of the chief fears that has kept her Medial Woman at bay is the fear that if she entered the mysteries of psyche, she would be swept up in turbulent forces and never return. This part of her resonates to Heraclitus's observation that one cannot go back, cannot step into the same river twice. Who we were, in the first plunge, has died or is dying. What she once believed about who she is, and how intimate she is willing to be, shifts. She outgrows the chrysalis which has kept her protected.

World Weary Woman realizes that her fear of life has kept her distanced from intimacy. With her penchant for potentiality, she is most comfortable dabbling with the mysteries when it comes to birth. She is not accustomed to linking death with intimacy. With a personal history containing so many traumatic losses (death and other), she has chosen to mask her pain with ambition, with new projects, goals, campaigns. Her attempt to keep Medial Woman's mysteries at a distance creates a barrier. But one day she learns, as Sandra put it, "to keep my finger no longer in the dike. I am drowning in a sea of things."

Sandra's words took me back to a time when I was drowning in my own sea of things. To complete my research for this book, I went to Egypt to study important hieroglyphs.

Because my bags have been lost on plane trips, it's been my practice to pack only carry-on luggage. On that particular journey, however, my companion and the airline agent convinced me that my carry-on must go with the rest of the cargo. Assured that the airline would be responsible, I surrendered. You can guess the end of the story. Mine was the only luggage missing when we arrived. Seven days later, my suitcase turned up. By then, the clothes I wore could nearly walk to me each morning. I had a toothbrush, but that was pretty much it. The temperature was upward of 115 degrees F. I became intimate with my own sweat, grime and body waste in a way I had never imagined. I can tell you that my appreciation for the conditions of the natives, including their poverty, grew exponentially. Ironically, so did my appreciation of their wealth. This is not to sentimentalize squalor. But it was in these conditions of no apparent relief that I began to notice wealth in a different way—the way known through the ages to Medial Woman. I was reminded that outer wealth vanishes, but the enduring treasure resides within. Medial Woman knows this.

When I arrived at my little room, a previous pilgrim had left behind the remnants of a small blue candle, with seven matches. A peach was on the dark wooden table beside the matches, as well as a few sheets of writing paper. In a drinking glass was a somewhat aging red hibiscus. A feast had been prepared, or so it seemed. For the next week I decided to budget that paper and candle, and indulge myself in whatever came from the foreign situation. Each day I arose before dawn, with the birds and creatures as my alarm clock. The lizards on the walls were especially effective as wake-up calls. On one such morning, I went across the Nile to a tiny village, en route to the tombs for my work. It was so early that the black wild dogs that roam the desert were still asleep. Suddenly, in the distance, I heard a muffled cry and saw flickering candles. Closer and closer came dark female forms of all ages, chanting, wailing in ways that move the marrow. Without knowing, something in me knew these women and their task. They were bearing the body of a dead child. The women were the women in the dream I had had the night before my son was killed six years earlier, women I'd never seen in waking life until this morning on the River Nile.

There is something that happens to a body and a soul when we are marked by such experiences. We realize we are alone, yet not alone. We realize we are a part of something much bigger than we had imagined, yet we share an intimacy with people whose names we may never know. We can both relate to and embrace their joys and sorrows as we bear witness to the life force itself, ebbing and flowing. It is as if that "central casting" archetype that Jung termed the Self sends into our lives the very bits and pieces we need, yet could not have fathomed on our own; all a part of the transcendent to which we each belong.

On my last morning in Africa, I returned to the banks of the Nile. The full moon hovered over native huts. Before dawn, my African sisters returned to the river's shore across from me—this time not in black but shades of clear yellow, orange, red, magenta, cobalt blue and turquoise. I had lost nothing, but gained their precious portrait, a portrait that shall go with me all the days of my life, enriching me in ways for which I lack all words.

As I returned to my room, the door was ajar. There, inside, was my orphaned suitcase, packed with things "I couldn't do without," but did.

Don't get me wrong. It was nice to have a fresh change of underwear, especially on my "every other day" when underneath my dress I wore nothing while my underthings dried. But the truth is, there is something oppressive about the weight of possessions which have, in the final analysis, so little to do with the treasure that endures.

Nonetheless, I am a practical woman and took my suitcase with me. Too bad, perhaps, for the story would seem more romantic if I could tell you I let it go. But my path is more and more about letting go of the romantic way of living and taking on the ordinary. What I can tell you is that my suitcase never seemed so heavy as on that return home, and that these days I travel lighter. Medial Woman was with me then, and has never entirely left. When Medial Woman is awakened in we World Weary Women, she comes to help. But the Amazon in us is suspicious; we want to know, as Maria Theresa put it on her first session:

> Why bother? I'm afraid to let go what I don't need. I feel a sort of hopelessness in the sorting. What do I need? What don't I need? I thought I knew, but I don't. Sorting takes so long. I want answers fast. I want guarantees, want you to tell me how many sessions will this take exactly? What will it cost me? Even though I know intellectually there is no certainty, inwardly I am outraged there is no way to know. Maybe the real problem is I don't know the first thing about how to trust, especially while in this abyss!

As Maria Theresa and others like her begin to flex and tone the trusting muscles of their Medial Woman, with slowly growing courage they can face whatever life's dance brings—deep sorrow, profound joy—not as enemies, but as allies. Working on trust, their symbolic life affects their receptivity to intimacy.

Glicca, the only daughter of an elderly couple, came with her parents and three brothers to the United States from Italy in 1949. Her grandparents, Italian and Lithuanian Jews, died in the death camps. Never married, Glicca became the school teacher her parents wanted. But she wearied of the increasing classroom size and decreasing benefits. After twelve years, she returned to school at age thirty-eight and became a successful corporate attorney at age forty-one, having taught school to manage her expenses.

By age fifty-two, Glicca was winning awards for activities that helped her community. This was not easy, as she was the sole care provider of her widowed mother, who had Alzheimer's disease. When the strain became too great, Glicca entered analysis to explore how she might cope. Highly motivated, Glicca pursued her symbolic world through her dream material in a deeply devoted way. Glicca takes Medial Woman seriously. Glicca radiates life. She is a full participant and has a magnetic attraction to anyone of like spirit. In 1996, at age fifty-nine, Glicca met her future husband one day when she was early for a session and chanced to go for tea while she reflected on her current life. As she laughingly put it:

> My Moshe was waiting for me all the time. I just had to learn to take myself seriously before God could give His clearance for us to meet. Now we are a couple of kids. Who would have thought it possible for old Glicca?

When we last spoke, Glicca was celebrating her sixty-third birthday in Israel with her sweetheart Moshe, seventy-eight.

This might seem confusing. What possible link could there be between learning to trust your inner symbolic life and interpersonal relatedness? Jung noted that the unconscious turns whatever face to us that we have shown to it. This is born out in my work with World Weary Woman. As she enriches her relationship to her inner bridegroom, as portrayed through dreams and creative work, she increases her compassion for her partner in everyday life. I have observed that the more World Weary Woman discovers what enhances her love of life, as opposed to that which diminishes her sense of well-being, she realizes she cannot go on in situations which deplete her. She begins to reconnect with her power to discern as she reconnects with her instincts. There is a paradoxical relationship here. The more she trusts her instinctive wisdom, a function of the feminine, the more her masculine side, her animus, functions as servant to her womanhood.

Discernment is a masculine function, a Logos attribute. As Glicca began to sort out what her dream figures were suggesting, she began to appreciate the natural law alive within her own being which was trying to help her. She said:

> Imagine the ultimate courtroom. In it you have a really fine judge. Maybe that's the Self. Then you have the attorneys, analogous to the ego, hoping for a good, healthy outcome. And you have the jury that is composed of parts of the psyche that's listening to evidence that is distorted by natural distortions of each witness's point of view. But this jury is the check and balance that requires consensus. That's what I'm trying to do in this depth work: Arrive at consensus between what I don't know about myself and what I do. I want to be unified, whole. I love Moshe. But, I

> cannot get whole from Moshe. He reflects how I feel about me. If I'm grumpy, I see him grumpy. If I am loving toward me, toward my life, chances are good I'll appreciate something I love about him and he feels this openness to his spirit, whether I put it into words or not.

Glicca's appreciation for the power of the unconscious in shaping outer reality as a reflection of the inner helps her hold a point of consciousness in her relationship with self, Moshe and others. Perhaps I am inspired by her capacity to make this connection, because so few in our world can. To do so means to give up blame and manipulation. Let's face it, we like to take the easiest road. Perhaps this accounts for the fact that blame is such a popular pursuit. As Tess, a teenager, pointed out the other day:

> It seems like the older I get, the more I feel like I'm expected to be a piece of machinery that fits into this huge machine, which has no interest in differences. My teachers, parents and even friends want me to be same, same, same, same old thing that they think they should be, whatever. But I'm not them, now, am I? Why does this piss them off so much? I don't know where I fit. My mom says I'll outgrow this stage, but I'm not so sure!

I include Tess's words because they are echoed again and again in the stories of World Weary Women, old enough to be mother and grandmother to Tess. Somewhere in between her discovery of how exhausted she is and her anger over what she has lost along the road to ambition, she awakens to how mechanical she has become in her dealings with those she loves most. This is a sickening realization. With the enormity of the isolation staring her in the face, World Weary Woman reaches a place in her journey when she exclaims: "I can't go on this way anymore!" Her protest comes from a body awareness. The more she recognizes what is possible through living symbolically, the less she is satisfied to live mechanically, intellectually. She wants intimacy. She craves creative community, innovative responses to what is in her heart. She feels the call to reconnect. She yearns to cherish, to be cherished.

The Hetaira

At this juncture, the Hetaira archetype comes to life in World Weary Woman. Wolff described this feminine structural form as

> instinctively related to the personal psychology of the male, and also to that of her children if she is married. The individual interests, inclina-

> tions and, possibly, also the problems of the male are within her conscious field of vision and are stimulated and promoted by her. She will convey to him the sense of a personal value quite apart from collective values, for her own development demands of her to experience and realize an individual relationship in all its nuances and depths. Schuré's "femmes inspiratrices" belong mainly to this structural form. . . . The function of the Hetaira is to awaken the individual psychic life in the male and to lead him through and beyond his male responsibilities towards the formation of a total personality. . . . Usually this development becomes the task of the second half of life. . . .
>
> The Hetaira thus affects the shadow side of the male and the subjective side of his Anima—a problem which is not without its danger. Consequently she ought to be, and at best is indeed, conscious of the laws of relationship. Her instinctive interest is directed towards the individual contents of a relationship in herself as well as in the man. For the man, a relationship in all its potentialities and nuances is usually less conscious and less important, for it distracts him from his tasks. For the Hetaira, it is decisive. Everything else—social security, position, etc.—is unimportant. In this lies both the significance and danger of the Hetaira. If she overlooks the Persona side of the man, . . . or adapts herself too blindly to it, she is bound to idolize the personal element, to incite it excessively and may bring the man to a point where he himself loses his clear vision of outer reality.[20]

But there is another danger, an even greater one to World Weary Woman. Not only can her man lose his clear vision of outer reality, but she can lose hers! When this happens, she loses her connection to herself. This would not be the first time. World Weary Woman has a history of losing herself in relationships with men, not the least of which was her father. Trying to please Daddy as a little girl, to keep him home, she courted his attention, played the inspiratrice. It failed to produce the effect she sought. She recalls his leaving, often when needed most. When he left her side, something in her died from sorrow. Said Glicca:

> I vowed I'd take care of myself. Every man I trusted seemed to have more important things to do than take me seriously. They were men who had important things to do. They were men of the world. Maybe that's a little part of why I became a lawyer. If they wouldn't come into my real world, I'd go to theirs, meeting them on their own terms, find what's so damn

---

[20] Ibid., pp. 7ff.

important out there to take them away from home. With men like that, you fade into the woodwork, whether you chase after them or not. They simply do not know you exist unless your center of attention is exclusively on their comfort. Even then, you are only a means to an end. This is what makes Moshe so different. He seems to notice that I am a human being, not a means to his satisfaction. Perhaps he reflects the simple fact that I was shifting how I saw myself when we met: from an object to a person with needs, feelings, and heart. Before my relationship with Moshe, which followed the shift in how I saw myself, I was both jealous and resentful of those women who seem to attract men like bees to honey, without so much as lifting a finger. Sometimes I still am envious. They seem to float into the room with an uncanny presence that melts men. I both want to know how they do it, and am repelled.

This is a repeating story in interviews with World Weary Women. How is it, she asks herself privately, that this other type of woman can glide so naturally into a room, effortlessly capturing the hearts of men without lifting a finger? She is intrigued and enraged, wishing and hopeless that such a fate could be hers. She argues that to be such a woman would be false for her. World Weary Woman insists if she were softer, she would be a fake. The truth is she is afraid.

But afraid of what? Union is World Weary Woman's goal and nemesis. Anna had such a dream when she was forty-eight:

I am in a room with many people. My husband and I have come to a seminar about marriage. The male speaker, in a very fancy suit, is lecturing on what makes relationships work. He is one of those slick guys you see in the movies—an Adonis. He is telling the women that they need to submit—to do whatever will please their man. Suddenly the scene shifts a little. Now I am with two of my good friends. I stand to speak in response to the man lecturing us. But as I do, my friends stand also. Our microphones are all interconnected. I cannot get heard clearly. Then something odd happens. The women with our triplet cord disappear and I am with my husband. We are watching two monkeys groom each other. We both laugh. We are enjoying the whole experience. I awaken puzzled, but happy.

When it comes to intimacy, World Weary Woman is accustomed to listening to the rules, recipes and opinions of outer authority. She both wants and fears a simpler, less authoritarian way. She is not comfortable with either her "monkey mind" (as Buddhists refer to the beginner's mind) or with "monkeying around." The way of the monkey can lead her home. Not the least interested in ambition, her monkey nature could care less about earning the proverbial gold watch which conventional living promises, as it promised Anna's father. But he died first.

For World Weary Woman to make contact with who she naturally is, she must confront her tendency to disconnect from her monkey body. She must learn to value her body and its monkey ways. My own mother, at times of stress, advised my sister and I to "rise above it." Unfortunately, her effort to teach us to extricate our focus from pettiness was heard as "disregard your body wisdom." Many women of her generation, and my grandmother's, were advised to do likewise. This has caused us to lose contact with instinctual knowing. The fact is, we cannot transform if we leave out our body. We need our physical body to partner with our spiritual body if we are ever to feel whole.

Such is the heart of intimacy. The English roots of the word, as far back as 1632, refer to "making known, deep seated." How can our personalities develop and grow if our spiritual body does not make itself known to our physical body, or our physical body does not communicate its nature to the spiritual? Wholeness requires this union of opposites, a union of greatest tension.

As World Weary Woman's Hetaira emerges and she becomes vulnerable to love, she fears the disappearance of the one she loves. More than a few have acknowledged something like this. Here are Glicca's words:

> One of the most frightening parts of loving Moshe was the inevitability of losing him. Sooner or later, one of us will leave. Either we'll get sick of each other and leave that way, or more likely, one of us will die first. I hope it's me who goes first. I've been the one who got left behind and I hate it. The one who leaves or dies has it easy. They're gone. Period. But, when you are the one still left, part of you dies, too.

Fear of Impermanence

Because World Weary Woman has such an extensive history of loss, she has reason to be anxious about loving and leaving. Her experience with life's impermanence has made her hesitant to enter intimate contact. For she knows that sorrow is as inevitable as joy. To join into a fully whole union with her partner, be it physically, emotionally or psychospiritually, she must accept the death that comes with such submission. We do not experience the transcendent without surrendering our ego's need to be in charge. Depth work does not take us to a candy shop. We Weary Ones might wish that we could have only sweetness from here on in. If only growth did not demand sacrifice! But, as we know full well, it does.

We Weary People are moving into a new relationship with the feminine. We are no longer allowed to "rise above" our innate body wisdom. If we persist in denying the imperative of the repressed feminine, we are confronted with the consequences of falling asleep.

We, the World Weary, sooner or later are called upon to honor the Hetaira within, to become truly the companion of the Self, surrendering to those conditions the universe brings to our door, using them as grist for the mill of individuation. World Weary Woman is called to a condition of expanded intimacy. The deeper this intimacy within, the more it affects outer relationships.

One of the most frightening aspects of deepened intimacy is that World Weary Woman must detach from her need for independence. As a defense against vulnerability, she has confused vulnerability with weakness. Her Amazon nature thrives when it feels autonomous. If she opens herself to intimacy, will her hard won freedom be usurped? Will she lose ground? Will she be left the fool? These are issues her ego raises as a red flag each time she finds herself yearning for spontaneous play, for "monkeying around." Her ego says to do so is foolish. The ego is fearful of this trickster nature of the psyche, which makes hopping about like a monkey appealing at times. Ego is hesitant toward anything wild, unbridled, natural.

But what the conscious mind can limit, the unconscious can invite. It is interesting that Anna's dream uses monkeys to make its point. I was reminded during my trip to Africa, especially in the Egyptian tombs, that there is a very different meaning of the monkey if we examine the ancient hieroglyphs. There, the symbol of the monkey as Thoth conveys creation. The monkey is needed by the Creator in order to record God's words (Ptah), attend to the evolution of life, and guide souls through the underworld. In travels to Mexico, I found parallels. Monkeys are connected to artists and artisans. Some years ago, while in the Orient, I was told that monkeys are related to creative powers which protect new life from hostile intrusion.

Returning to the monkey dream, then, we could say that on the collective level, the dreamer was being shown by the Self that her intimacy issue might be improved if she learns to cherish her monkey nature, for this grooming can assist the development of the new personality her Self intends to create—who she was destined to become from the beginning.

Destined To Become

World Weary Woman seems to question the most who she is destined to become through her struggle with intimacy. As she releases her need to be other than she is, and can accept the fact that her shadow contains something fertile and renewing as well as fetid and destroying, her outer relations become more serene, less extreme. Whatever comes, World Weary Woman finds within herself a deeper capacity to hold it in an intimate, compelling way. The demands of such intimacy are profound and moving.

I am reminded of Claire, fifty-six at the time of her original interview. She longed for an intimate partner. Several years later, she and Jerry found each other. Theirs was a love affair of life's autumn. Shortly after they married, he died suddenly of cancer. Not only did they share a rich love, they also faced life's end squarely, living intimately with each moment's hello and good-bye. Since Jerry's death, Claire now faces a new demand: that of letting him go, allowing herself to grieve from her depths—a privilege and necessity not given her at the age of five when her mother died suddenly from appendicitis.

The Self requires Claire to visit these dark places, bringing her adult and child nature as companions to her suffering heart. Her adult intellect understands and appreciates what she's had, and that loss is part of life. But her child nature simply hurts, and is afraid. As Claire brings consciousness to her dreams about her husband, the part of her that has been grieving since she was five becomes affirmed, received. She is given an opportunity and space to hold close what is precious, and to reenter life.

Claire is sixty-eight now. Her evolving story, like those of the other World Weary Women with whom I work, continues to teach me.

World Weary Woman's Archetypal Play

As she transits through life's events, World Weary Woman's personality develops in tandem with the degree of consciousness she brings to her relationship with the Self. During a period when I was desperately trying to formulate this progression in a linear way, I fell asleep at my writing table and had this dream:

> I am shown a very large theater in the round. Center stage is a woman who is in costume as an Amazon. She is confident, assertive, hardworking, well-toned, and active in the world. She has strength, presence.

> But this is not a stationary stage. The light changes as the stage begins to rotate. Another character that has been in the wings is rotated to center stage, in a very maternal Demeter type costume. She is suckling a child. Her entire focus is on the new life in her arms as she nurses. After sufficient pause, the stage rotates several more times, to an "otherworldly" artist-type woman, who works in a very inwardly-attuned visionary/mystical way, with mysterious materials; and finally, the fourth is a woman gowned in a very sensual, satin gown. I had the sense that central to all four was the unseen presence of the choreographer of this entire dance cycle. It was there, transcending each of the characters, yet unifying, directing and creating the story. At no time were the characters missing. Although one might be holding the spotlight the others were present, even if hidden from sight.

I knew this to be a metaphor for World Weary Woman's portrait.

Here is a progressive cycle. World Weary Woman develops through the interplay of her personal life with archetypal contents, some of which are brought to light. But whether or not she is conscious of these forces, they are alive and working in her. As she, and we, do the work which becoming conscious demands, we bear witness to emerging authenticity. To the degree that she can awaken to these powerful archetypal forces and sort out her personal identity from them, not only can her ego strength grow, but also her relationship to the totality of herself becomes enriched. Just as the main character in a play does not interact with all other roles simultaneously, lest there be excessive chaos, World Weary Woman, as a healthy personality, encounters her feminine archetypes in a cyclical way.

Even after many interviews and analytic work with World Weary Women, I know of no way to predict just how long or under what circumstances each archetypal coupling will come, or how long it will last. Nor can it be controlled. But what World Weary Woman can do is bring consciousness to whatever arises. If she allows this natural movement, her ability to incorporate energy from each encounter not only increases her ego strength and sense of who she is naturally in her world, it also enhances her vitality. As she brings consciousness to bear witness to what is seizing her attention, this progression of archetypal encounters offers her the change to deepen her contact with the Self.

The truth is that every woman contains these archetypes. As World Weary Woman confronts the way in which her overidentification with her Amazon has left her depleted, this seems to lead her to the discovery of other ways of expressing her unlived life. As we have found, although she exhibits Amazon tendencies when most stressed, we cannot say she *is* the Amazon. To do so would be analogous to believing an actress is only the role she happens to be acting at the moment.

In the ten years since we began this study, participants have described an increasing awareness of their private loneliness, their longing for warmth and intimacy beneath their Amazon. This desire includes the yearning for interpersonal intimacy, even though World Weary Woman struggles with feelings described by one as "incompetent, adolescent fumbling for the right thing to do or say when I'm with someone that I care for." When she turns to the outer world to enact intimacy, she finds, as one said, "I lose myself when I get swallowed up in who he wants or needs me to be for him to be happy."

Frustrated, she moves toward intimacy with others, but cannot get there directly without developing it with the Self. When she can no longer run from what she feels when this happens, she begins to turn inward for nourishment, often as an outcome of her therapeutic work. Here, if fortunate, she finds contact with herself in a nurturing atmosphere. She struggles to connect with a cherishing, patient Mother archetype within herself. That she finds encouragement in the way of the feminine comes as a surprise, of which she may be suspicious. She has little history with such a possibility. Nonetheless, the warmth of relatedness in her outer world seems a necessary element before she can descend into her own interior landscape with compassion and forgiveness for herself.

As World Weary Woman dares the descent into her own depths, she confronts the irrational Medial Woman who understands those great mysteries that are often unvalued in the outer world. As she grows more comfortable with Medial Woman's way of symbolic living, she finds increased spaciousness within herself, leaving her better equipped to reach out in tender mercy and tolerance to others, a by-product of withdrawing projections. It is at these times that her appreciation of Albert Einstein's purported remark can blossom: "At the end of my life my greatest discovery is to find that the world is a friendly place after all."

Much of World Weary Woman's struggle seems to be one of finding a way to mediate between these archetypal opposites: the Amazon and Medial Woman, both impersonally related, and the Mother and Hetaira, personally related. As she undulates around and among these dichotomies, she slowly discovers that another force supports this dance, the intent of which is self-realization. World Weary Woman spins downward, round and round the spindle of Self, in order to find her own connection to wholeness.

We find in this an echo of Jung's discovery that at the core of any complex there is an archetype—a pervasive, cross-cultural pattern within the collective unconscious. But there is also an "archetype of archetypes," so to speak, a regulating center in the psyche that Jung called the Self. It is the Self from which unique individuality emerges. This Self is purposeful in seeking expression and fulfillment.

Warmth as Safety

The stories of World Weary Woman illustrate the self-regulating function of the Self at work in soma and psyche. Anna, mentioned earlier, is a fifty-year-old African-American unmarried stockbroker whose blood pressure was climbing in a dangerous way. She was told by family and friends to "slow down, relax . . ." To this, she and her World Weary sisters respond privately:

> It isn't that I don't know what to do or even what I should eliminate in my schedule in order to relax. The problem is I don't know how. I don't know how to let go of things that seem important to others, or they need me to do; and I don't know how to say what I need.

For World Weary Woman, there is an enormous gulf between understanding the therapeutic advice she is given, and its application. For instance, after Anna suffered cardiac symptoms of a frightening magnitude, she put it this way: "Maybe I've been moving faster than my angels can fly." The advice to slow down suggests that to do so is simple. However, even though she makes a conscious decision to do so, the unconscious side of her nature resists.

Slowing down means coming to a new depth of intimacy with herself. World Weary Woman can find such an encounter terrifying. Although connecting with her soul is a prerequisite for her wholeness, she does not move directly toward it. She comes to her true ground in a meandering way. World Weary Woman requires safety before she can receive such a gift. The most oft-repeated word which connotes safety by her definition is "warmth." As she gravitates toward it, she moves closer to the Mother archetype, both within herself and in the world. This takes time.

One woman describes the process like this: "Letting my guard down is something I do only a little bit at a time. It is as if I am peeking out from behind this armor until there is the right opening and I can let down and take in." After a series of disheartening experiences she concluded: "Others can turn on you when you've just bared your soul . . . so I've learned to be tough as nails."

It takes patience for World Weary Woman to access the nourishment and rest required. Historically, she has trusted the world of Logos more than that of Eros. Here she is on new soil. Each time she receives mothering from herself and others, she feels better equipped to descend into deeper, symbolic realms. When she makes such a leap, she meets the world of the irrational.

Entry into the World of the Feminine

The Medial Woman is that aspect of a woman's nature that helps her mediate between the world of the feminine, with its symbolic way of living, and the masculine outer world of reason and results. As the bridge is formed between her ego and Self, she begins moving, literally and figuratively, in a more flowing, rhythmic, intimate and heartfelt way, as a lover of life. She finds her Hetaira, tiny step by tiny step. Just as we do not develop our most neglected muscles and inferior functions directly, but must move slowly through a side door, she does not at first develop the side of herself she has resisted so strongly.

World Weary Woman's return to living in a more meaningful way involves her return to her own feeling nature. Without this, she cannot connect to the events of her life in a way that brings renewed vitality, much less meaning. She is critical of her feelings and instincts, mistrusting her own values. As she strives for consciousness, this harshness lessens.

The Self requires a particular atmosphere for it to express itself most fruitfully. This is strongly shaped by the parents' presence or absence. But not only does the child have its personal parents, she also has the parental archetypes in her psyche. These are activated as she interacts with her environment, and they shape her perception.

4
World Weary Woman's Journey

The Split As Seen in Enduring Stories

Perhaps one reason why Jung told the story of the Rainmaker again and again is that World Weary People who have embarked upon their journey of self-discovery can relate to it. Here it is, as Jung heard it from the famous Sinologist Richard Wilhelm, translator of the *I Ching:*

The Rainmaker

> There was a great drought where Wilhelm lived; for months there had not been a drop of rain and the situation became catastrophic. The Catholics made processions, the Protestants made prayers, and the Chinese burned joss-sticks and shot off guns to frighten away the demons of the drought, but with no result. Finally the Chinese said "We will fetch the rain-maker." And from another province a dried up old man appeared. The only thing he asked for was a quiet little house somewhere, and there he locked himself in for three days. On the fourth day the clouds gathered and there was a great snow-storm at the time of the year when no snow was expected, an unusual amount, and the town was so full of rumors about the wonderful rain-maker that Wilhelm went to ask the man how he did it. In true European fashion he said "They call you the rain-maker, will you tell me how you made the snow?" And the little Chinese said: "I did not make the snow, I am not responsible." "But what have you done these three days?" "Oh, I can explain that. I come from another country where things are in order. Here they are out of order, they are not as they should be by the ordinance of heaven. Therefore the whole country is not in Tao, and I am also not in the natural order of things because I am in a disordered country. So I had to wait for three days until I was back in Tao and then naturally the rain came."[21]

It is easy to fall out of harmony with our center, our soul. Such a disharmony manifests in our lives symbolically through time frustrations: too much to do. It is hard to relax when we are pushed so hard to produce. This is not a fantasy. A recent study described in June, 2000, by *ABC News,* showed that Americans work longer hours than the people in any

[21] *Mysterium Coniunctionis,* CW 14, par. 604, note 211.

country in the Western world, with less vacation. On average, Americans work two months more per year than Germans, and two weeks longer than the Japanese. So when Anna tells us that she is "moving faster than her angels can fly," and that she knows she should relax and let go, but does not know how, she is not alone. We can learn techniques. But nothing changes if we do not make that fundamental shift in the underlying attitude which propels the drive to produce. Disengaged from the Tao, or central place of fertile calm within the psyche, we spin faster and faster until something more powerful stops us in our tracks.

As I listened to World Weary Woman's story, through all her voices, it was tempting to write off her race going nowhere as a by-product of modern times. Articles abound which suggest such a view, as do self-help books. I, too, have been guilty of romanticizing the past, but when I look at the facts of my parents', grandparents' and great grandparents' lives, I can see that this conclusion is inadequate. My people have always been hard workers, with little reprieve. Maybe this is true in your ancestral roots as well.

But what is possible is to explore the collective history of you, Anna, me and other World Weary Women, by looking at enduring stories which are not only reported cross-culturally, but have stood the test of time. Initially, this might be difficult for the Amazon. Investing attention in story might seem another waste of time. This is often the case in preliminary work with World Weary Women. We may feel impatient, irritated, mistrusting; silently or not so silently demanding, "But what does this have to do with me?" After all, she is not an archetype. She is a human being with flesh, blood and feelings. Pausing demands a leap of faith for World Weary Woman.

The importance of having the correct attitude, one that is unhurried and centered, that enables a connection with the Self, is suggested in fairy tale, folk lore, mythology and family stories passed from one generation to the next.

"Mother Holle"

A number of these enduring stories of redemption from suffering involve a well. Because the symbolic well is so important as a healing image for the psyche, it is not surprising that there is reference to it as an important vehicle for transformation of human suffering. The tale we will use as a connecting thread for the transformation of World Weary Woman is "Mother Holle" or "Frau Holle." The Grimm Brothers collected a number of versions from different countries. While there are some differences, the underlying motifs are the same.

Mother Holle

There was once a widow who had two daughters—one of whom was pretty and industrious, whilst the other was ugly and idle. But she was much fonder of the ugly and idle one, because she was her own daughter; and the other, who was a stepdaughter, was obliged to do all the work, and be the Cinderella of the house. Every day the poor girl had to sit by a well, in the highway, and spin and spin till her fingers bled.

Now it happened that one day the spindle was marked with her blood, so she dipped it in the well, to wash the mark off; but it dropped out of her hand and fell to the bottom. She began to weep, and ran to her stepmother and told her of the mishap. But she scolded her sharply, and was so merciless as to say: "Since you have let the spindle fall in, you must fetch it out again."

So the girl went back to the well, and did not know what to do; and in the sorrow of her heart she jumped into the well to get the spindle. . . .

She lost her senses, and when she awoke and came to herself again, she was in a lovely meadow where the sun was shining and many thousands of flowers were growing. Across this meadow she went, and at last came to a baker's oven full of bread, and the bread cried out: "Oh, take me out! Take me out! Or I shall burn; I have been baked a long time!" So she went up to it, and took out all the loaves one after another with the bread-shovel. After that she went on till she came to a tree covered with apples, which called out to her: "Oh, shake me! We apples are all ripe!" So she shook the tree till the apples fell like rain, and went on shaking till they were all down, and when she had gathered them into a heap, she went on further.

At last she came to a little house, out of which an old woman peeped; but she had such large teeth that the girl was frightened, and was about to run away. But the old woman called out to her: "What are you afraid of, dear child? Stay with me; if you will do all the work in the house properly, you shall be the better for it. Only you must take care to make my bed well, and to shake it thoroughly till the feathers fly—for then there is snow on the earth. I am Mother Holle."

As the old woman spoke so kindly to her, the girl took courage and agreed to enter her service. She attended to everything to the satisfaction of her mistress, and always shook her bed so vigorously that the feathers flew about like snow-flakes. So she had a pleasant life with her; never an angry word; and to eat she had roast meat every day.

She stayed some time with Mother Holle, before she became sad. At first she did not know what was the matter with her, but found at length that it was home-sickness: although she was many thousand times better off here than at home, still she had a longing to be there. At last she said to the old woman: "I have a longing for home; and however well off I am down here, I cannot stay any longer; I must go up again to my own people." Mother Holle said: "I am pleased that you long for your home again, and as you have served me so truly, I myself will take you up again." Thereupon she took her by the hand, and led her to a large door. The door was opened, and just as the maiden was standing beneath the doorway, a heavy shower of golden rain fell, and all the gold clung to her, so that she was completely covered over with it.

"You shall have that because you have been so industrious," said Mother Holle; and at the same time she gave her back the spindle which she had let fall into the well. Thereupon the door closed, and the maiden found herself up above the earth not far from her mother's house.

And as she went into the yard the cock was sitting on the well, and cried: "Cock-a-doodle-doo! Your golden girl's come back to you!" So she went in to her mother, and as she arrived there covered with gold, she was well received, both by her and her sister.

The girl told all that had happened to her, and as soon as the mother heard how she had come by so much wealth, she was very anxious to obtain the same good luck for the ugly and lazy daughter. She had to seat herself by the well and spin; and in order that her shuttle might be stained with blood, she stuck her hand into a thorn bush and pricked her finger. Then she threw her spindle into the well, and jumped in after it.

She came, like the other, to the beautiful meadow and walked along the very same path. When she got to the oven the bread again cried: "Oh, take me out! Take me out! Or I shall burn; I have been baked a long time!" But the lazy thing answered: "As if I had any wish to make myself dirty!" and on she went. Soon she came to the apple-tree, which cried: "Oh, shake me! Shake me! We apples are all ripe!" But she answered: "I like that! One of you might fall on my head," and so went on. When she came to Mother Holle's house she was not afraid, for she had already heard of her big teeth, and she hired herself to her immediately.

The first day she forced herself to work diligently, and obeyed Mother Holle when she told her to do anything, for she was thinking of all the gold that she would give her. But on the second day she began to be lazy, and on the third day still more so, and then she would not get up in the morning at all. Neither did she make Mother Holle's bed as she ought, and did not shake it so as to make the feathers fly up. Mother Holle was soon tired of this, and gave her notice to leave. The lazy girl was willing enough to go, and thought that now the golden rain would come. Mother Holle led her also to the great door; but while she was standing beneath it, instead of the gold a big kettle full of pitch was emptied over her. "That is the reward for your service," said Mother Holle, and shut the door.

So the lazy girl went home, but she was quite covered with pitch, and the cock on the well, as soon as he saw her, cried out: "Cock-a-doodle-doo! Your dirty girl's come back to you!" But the pitch clung fast to her, and could not be got off as long as she lived.[22]

The tale takes place somewhere in the past. After the introduction, we find the pretty sister (called Gold Marie in the German version) alone at the well spinning. Her Amazon is at work. By the end, the characters are joined by Mother Holle beneath the well, and the cock above. Thus, at the beginning the masculine is missing and the feminine is grieving.

The interaction of archetypal components of this fairy tale brings about a series of so-called ups-and-downs in the unfolding of the story. How like life! Beginning with a feeling of "down," Gold Marie's situation worsens. We are not privy to her thoughts or feelings because she is an archetypal force, not a human being. But on the human level, who among us does not know this predicament? Her spinning at the well alone leaves her fingers bleeding, which marks the spindle. As she attempts to remove the mark of her suffering, her situation becomes worse, and the spindle drops into the well.

Imagine. Recall the sensation of such a situation. From this low point, there is a suggestion of upward movement when she turns to home for help. Maybe she bargains with herself that the situation might improve. Rejection of her plea brings her to collapse into tears, a lower point of suffering than before. Jumping into the well takes her to the bottom. As a natural consequence of descent, her suffering is brought to resolution. As she becomes supplicant, serving Mother Holle, the Great Mother, she reaps a reward. Even though she is nourished at the latter's home, we be-

---

[22] *The Complete Grimms' Fairy Tales,* pp. 133ff. (slightly modified).

come aware of yet another unanticipated twist of the plot—her homesickness. This heaviness is met by an equally unexpected turn of events—receiving the gold along with the spindle. The movement progresses in an upward fashion when she returns home with her found treasure, and is met by her family to whom she relates what happened. Their need for what she brings seems to allay another downward turn in her fate.

For the ugly sister (Tar Marie in the German version), however, there is a different unfolding. Indulged by her mother (stepmother to Gold Marie), she is crippled, unadapted to the outer world. Without awareness in how to function there, she falsifies her suffering to take a shortcut toward gaining treasure. Apparently, neither shortcuts nor cheating are new. She enters the world falsely, and does not know how to meet authentic nature. Because she refuses to serve nature, what begins for her as a journey of high hopes ends with disappointment, a downward turn. Her laziness in serving what transcends ego goals marks her fate with pitch. (I am left with the feeling that Tar Marie's story is not over, though her shadow sister's journey as Gold Marie seems complete with transformation.)

Comparative Material

In the first few lines of "Mother Holle," we find a comparison to the story of Cinderella. Much better known in America than "Mother Holle," it is a story referenced frequently by World Weary Woman. There is something familiar in the Cinderella theme of these tales to which World Weary Woman responds. Cinderella, too, is the orphan child left with a cruel stepmother and stepsisters. Her industry and beauty compensate her shadow sisters' ugliness and laziness. Through her innocent heart, like Gold Marie, she devotes herself to the tasks required of her, and this brings her to transformation. While she does not go on an underground voyage, she does meet nature in other ways, and is helped by the transcendent in the form of her fairy godmother. By the end of the tale she is in receipt of the kingdom through marriage. Her sisters, like Tar Marie, meet their own suffering as a direct result of their ambition, envy and greed.

"Cinderella" differs, however, in several important respects. It is set in the frame of royalty, wherein live a king, a queen and a prince. The male element is included through human forms. Also a royal marriage takes place, whereas this does not happen in "Mother Holle." As an aside, I have noted with interest that World Weary Woman mentions, not infrequently, her disillusionment in "my prince." More than a few have complained that their belief that they would find a "happy-ever-after" marriage has cost them dearly. Eventually, they come to the painful work of taking back these impossible projections on human men, which cannot be avoided if wholeness is to be gained and their relations transformed. But first they, like Gold Marie, Cinderella and the Greek maiden Persephone, must enter their own confrontation with Hades.

The myth of Persephone and Demeter contains important links to this tale as well. Although the two stories begin differently, both contain a theme of transformation of the Kore, or young maiden. One fundamental difference is that Persephone is with her mother, Demeter, in the beginning of her story. She has been protected until that fateful day when alone in the meadow, her captivation by a beautiful flower created a certain vulnerability whereby she could fall victim to her abduction by Hades. Although Persephone's father conspired with Hades to set up the rape, this is not so in the fairy tale. Both young women are affected by the absence of a helpful father; each left to mature through her journey into the Underworld. Both maidens begin their journey of feminine transformation by suffering. Each must contend with darkness and come to terms with the initial disorientation this brings before they can make new choices.

Whereas Persephone's mother searches for her, and Gold Marie's does not, we need to note that Mother Holle supports the latter's transformation as soon as she responds to nature with an open heart. I am reminded here of a statement attributed to Julian of Norwich: "No one looks for God who has not already found Him."[23] Paraphrasing this, we might say that a woman does not look for Mother Nature in herself until she has already found Her in her heart. Just as we seek the Creator, Her Creation seeks us.

Although time and space limitations do not permit a full-scale comparison with all the tales that might amplify "Mother Holle," there is one category which must not be overlooked. This concerns itself with the theme of sibling rivalry, an issue present throughout human history and exemplified in the story of Cain and Abel. We see the power principle at work in Cain, who slays his brother Abel. But we can never obtain from another what resides in us. That it is an irritant to see our sibling radiate life in ways we have not cultivated is understandable. We are jealous of those who develop their potentialities when we do not. If we feel guilty

---

[23] Quoted by Helen Luke in *The Way of Woman.*

because we value worldly appearances more than the eternal, it is understandable that those who make different choices put us to the test. If we remain disconnected from the eternal within, self-doubt grows, as does envy. The deepest level of guilt, of course, stems from not taking responsibility for living life to the fullest. But it is easier to remain the unconscious victim, and to project our guilt as resentment. This is a common aspect of human nature.

In the Biblical tale of Mary and Martha the shadow is constellated in slightly different ways. Martha, the industrious sister, complains that Mary, the idler, should not be invited to sit at Jesus' feet. But she is told that there is a time for work and a time for other ways of being. Jesus seems to be elevating the value of Eros, or *chesed*, demonstrated by his ancestor Ruth. Indeed, had Ruth not followed her own way, into the dark and unfamiliar soil of a new life which led her to devoted service with a tender heart, her relatedness would not have culminated with the birth of a lineage leading to David, and, eventually, Jesus. Ruth, and others mentioned, were tested with their willingness to give up the comfortable in service of something greater than their own glorification in the eyes of others.

Because this tale begins with a trio of women, it is important to frame this within the context of another triune meeting of the feminine, which had to do with tender devotion to the "other" at the foot of the cross of Christ. There at Christ's feet waited three women who loved him and served him through Eros, each by the name of Mary. Like maiden, mother and crone in the story of Persephone, via the latter, Demeter and Hecate, we find the intermingling of women in service to transformation in the death/rebirth cycle of development. If we adapt such a trinity to the context of the fairy tale, we might find the widow flanked on either side by shadow sisters, Gold Marie and Tar Marie, each of whom reflects one reaction to suffering.

Consistently in the aforementioned stories, we find one simple truth: whenever an attitude interrupts progressive realization of the Self, a sacrifice is asked.

Framing the Problem

Were we to interpret "Mother Holle" alone, it could be said that it is an archetypal story of feminine transformation. Ambition must be sacrificed to meet nature's requirements for transformation. This means that we must enter into relationship with our unconscious with an attitude of devoted service to the Self, the task of the second half of life, rather than hold to ego goals, priorities in the first half. In this context the fairy tale deals with the issue of the shadow's crucial role in transformation. Here we are shown the problem of a beautiful, industrious Gold Marie, in her Amazon nature, juxtapositioned against her shadow sister, Tar Marie. Although it is traditionally not wise to mix levels in a fairy tale interpretation, let us transgress this injunction here, for our primary subject is the transformation of World Weary Woman where these archetypes have their influence.

Taken this way, we find another important archetypal shadow creature, her animus-possessed stepmother. She corresponds to negative Mother, whose sole agenda is power. This aspect of the unconscious is poor because she is unconnected to that very core of womanhood which is renewed by nature. It is also important to note that while stepmother rejects Gold Marie, it is this rejection that is instrumental in Gold Marie's journey to the Great Mother, where she receives wisdom through surrender. Therefore, the rejecting mother turns out to be crucial to Gold Marie's transformation because she forces Gold Marie to set out upon her own path to wholeness. While we might not like it, betrayal can precipitate growth. This is not to condone cruelty, but to say what is so.

Because the fairy tale brings us information psychologically about the interaction of archetypes from the collective psyche, we can apply what we find to the collective situation of World Weary Women. These collective forces contribute to World Weary Woman's difficulty. Deep within the shadowlands of her unconscious live archetypal characters interacting with one another. Although she might wish to go on believing she is boss in her own house or psyche, the fact is that unconscious forces exert powerful effects upon what she thinks and feels and how she behaves. The more unconscious she is, the more she not only becomes the medium through which they exert their power in shaping her fate, but the more she tries to identify with the light (good, industrious, beautiful) aspects of nature while disowning her shadow. It is this overidentification that leaves her depleted. Her weariness is the natural result of disregarding her own darkness, her unconscious, hidden motivations.

The fairy tale is not a story about an individual. Rather it is about archetypal forces that can take hold of us without our permission, or even awareness. Yet individual World Weary Woman's tendency is to overidentify with her Gold Marie, industriously spinning, and at times seeing herself as the heroine who is victimized by circumstance.

World Weary Woman is *not* Gold Marie. However, the characters in the story reflect an interaction well known within our psyche. She relates to the tale, to its archetypal interaction, even when she does not understand what it is that causes her strong attraction to or rejection of the story.

Much of World Weary Woman's redemption comes when she embraces these shadow aspects of nature. She must find her Gold Marie: that pure heart which can relinquish ambitious goals and learn to live simply, serving nature's requirements. So, too, is she faced with finding the truth of laziness when it comes to the care and feeding of her own soul, a task unvalued in her world. As this happens, she is left the task of reconciling with stepmother within, which prefers to disown any creative children not of her own planning. In short, World Weary Woman's task is to relinquish her spinning—that penchant for wishful thinking that leaves such an animus woman cut off from life.

A closer look at the story enriches this understanding and offers some suggestions about how the process of reconciliation occurs.

Elaboration

By the end of the first sentence of "Mother Holle," we have a story rich in description of the condition of our time. The fifth word is "poor" and the sixth is "widow." From the onset, then, we enter a predicament of grief-stricken, impoverished femininity. Loss sets the stage for its transformation The etymological Latin root of the word "poor" refers to depleted soil whereas "wealth" refers to a state of fertilization. In the fairy tale, then, we are presented with a "poor widow" (and her family) who live in a depleted atmosphere disconnected from the receptive ground of the feminine which is ripe with possibilities for renewed living. Thus, poverty reflects a severance from what enlivens and enriches body and soul, leaving each in bankruptcy. In short, "to be poor," connotes a state of the feminine suffering infertility. This is a condition known throughout history, reflected in the earliest Egyptian hieroglyphic accounts, and later through fairy tales and myths. "Mother Holle" is such a story.

How are we understand the heroine of this tale? Archetypal figures are pure forms, impersonal forces of the unconscious, living below personal complexes. The tale doesn't show us how the heroine feels. We are given what she *does.* It is we who must bring our own feelings and experience to such archetypal bones.

It is interesting that in the English translation the heroine lacks a name, leaving her in the realm of the ordinary. She is not royalty or of the aristocracy, but simply the stepdaughter of a poor widow. In the German version, however, she is given a name: Gold Mary or Gold Marie. Mary/Marie can be related to an aspect of Sophia and to the three Marys—the mother of Christ, the friend of Christ, or Mary Magdalene—the converted prostitute who not only resigns from the collective way, but becomes disciple and steward, the first to see Christ after resurrection. Mary as a name, therefore, could suggest the heroine has a certain consciousness, one who sees. This possibility is underscored by the other part of her name, "Gold." Gold suggests a solar quality to her nature, that is, a state of new beginnings through consciousness.

What does such a character actually *do* within the tale which might suggest more about her nature? Gold Marie does not sit at home like her shadow sister, but goes out into the world. There she spins industriously by the well. She is a hard worker who does not shirk her moral duty. We see her take courageous steps, daring the adventure of life, responding to nature's needs with an open and uncomplaining heart. That is the attitude of service which brings her the gold. Her outer state reflects the inner: she enriches life and is enriched by her relatedness.

The paradox is that while she becomes differentiated from the collective, she interacts, as archetype, within this world, and when these efforts are rewarded, wealth replaces a former state of impoverishment. Apparently this archetype has within it the capacity to cleave to inner wealth despite outer adversity. This may well have been the underlying message the Self was bringing Anna through her janitor dream related in chapter one. Recall that despite her industrious efforts, her dream-life custodian continued dumping trash on her desk She was hungry but did not feed herself, because she was worried about being more ambitious. She is reminded by her husband-animus that gold comes in many forms. She is looking for it in the wrong place.

Gold Marie returns home covered with the gold. Mother Holle has bestowed this treasure upon her for her service. But what is the meaning of such a gift from Great Mother? She is not spinning. She is not rushed. She is doing simply what is required: no more, no less. She responds to nature. Gold as the incorruptible metal, a solar element, reigns eternal in this state. Alchemically, the gold symbolizes that end state toward which the alchemists strove in their devotion. The task was one of distillation: to transform through a rigorous process of service what is leaden in matter, or "base," into the priceless treasure. The alchemists did not hurry. They did not clean up another's mess. They took the time necessary to conduct their search. Theirs, as Jung has told us, was a projective process whereby one's inner transformation was reflected back to them through their interrelationship with matter.

So the maiden covered with gold is the one whose devotion to serving nature has transformed and developed her personality through an evolved consciousness. Such an archetypal figure can be discerned through how she radiates.

On an intrapsychic level, this is the aspect of the analysand that "shines through" in a session, even though the content of what she shares may be murky or in a complete muddle. Archetypally, Gold Marie is the nugget of consciousness. This pure consciousness has a radiating effect. In the presence of those who find inner gold, we feel love, maybe even blessed. Transformation seems possible in such a warm atmosphere. Here, we feel met, accepted, cherished. When World Weary Woman accepts her nature, including her flaws, we feel more inclined to do likewise. I am reminded of Anna's words to me:

> I was taught that you shouldn't feel sorry for yourself. Lots of people come on hard times. What's the use of complaining? So, when Jesse died I had nowhere to go with it. Okay, my husband was dead. Lots of women lose their husbands. It is happening right now, while I'm talking to you. I've believed that if nothing helps, why bother talking about it? I thought I was supposed to get on with being a widow, get past the pain. I'm the one who's supposed to have the answers. That doesn't help either. I have questions, not answers. I'm mixed up. I don't know how to be a widow. Frankly, I doubt I'll ever feel finished with what I really feel.

Anna's courage to be real is invitational. Although I was transcribing her words, a part of me couldn't help but draw silent comparisons. As a bereaved mother, I am familiar with the pressure to move past loss. I, too, have felt mixed up at how to hold what I'd prefer not be part of my history. But Anna's genuine sharing, and others like her, has had an infectious affect on me. Drawing from her own deep well of truth, she inspires the same in me.

In "Mother Holle," such radiance is drawn from the place beneath the well, creation's centerpoint, where the feminine aspect of God resides. We are reminded that the source of wealth lives in realms we least expect, and mostly overlook, beneath our routine outlook. The divine lives in a domain deeper than reason. It operates in accord with its own laws. In this place, feathers must fly: inspiration is a necessity to keep creation going. The divine operates in its own way and realm.

This golden state is the outcome, not the inception, of the story. The story begins with the problem of poverty, and this is crucial to understanding. This state of loss, this feeling of darkness, sets the progression into motion. Not only has stepmother lost her husband, but the heroine has lost her father and, most immediately, her spindle. And it is the loss of this spindle which forces her to break away from the collective world (highway and stepfamily) and go inward to the ground of nature Herself.

This gives the spindle symbolic import. Practically speaking, the spinning wheel is used to transform raw material into a more refined aspect of nature as thread. The image itself has been tied mythologically to the Three Norns, or Three Fates. Sometimes referred to as Fate's daughters, the Moirae use the spindle to keep the cycle of life going: from past to present to future. Their spinning movement reflects the reality of birth, growth and the inevitability of death's approach, when Fate announces its pronouncement. If a spindle is lost, this intricate rhythm is broken. The loss of some vital link with life is the outcome. So it is the retrieval of this life-restoring spindle which catalyzes the adventure.

And what is the adventure psychologically? It is possible to take the heroine as an impulse from the unconscious which seeks reunion with natural life. Waters of the unconscious must be plumbed so that the new center of personality can transform itself from the depths of nature, and return to the conscious world with an enriched way of living. As this consciousness arrives, other aspects of the psyche, not yet redeemed, are alerted regarding this new development. This means that other aspects in the unconscious, shadowy elements such as complexes or animus, might be called to action. Because what we've not faced consumes energy, to harness this energy requires confrontation with parts of our nature we've not accepted.

Bit by bit, what we've rejected about ourselves begins to surface. If we are willing to do the work that self-examination requires, growth results.

Growth does not happen when there is ulterior motivation such as "getting gold." Gold Marie does not do what she does to get rich. She is rich because her service comes from a good heart. Her reward reflects her inner state. We of the Western world might take note of the fact that she does not take what she's been given to the marketplace. She is not interested in self-aggrandizing goals of fame. Gold Marie keeps life simple.

This brings up a question commonly voiced by World Weary Woman, although in different words. How does "grace" arrive in our lives? This cannot be predicted. We Weary Ones might hope that it is we who bring about the transformation. But is this so? Perhaps more than anything, the best we can do is set an invitational atmosphere in which grace may enter. If "she" does, transformation is the gift. But if grace keeps her distance, what is the best outcome we might expect? This is a question for which each must find a personal answer. In the meantime there is choice, even in the apparent absence of grace. Sometimes it seems that no answers come. This is discouraging. What to do? Well, we can do our best to receive what life brings each day with as much consciousness as can be mustered, responding to the best of our ability. Why some appear to "get the gold" with less work than others is a question to which I have no answer.

Nonetheless, what we can see in the tale is that it is not whim but necessity that spurs Gold Marie into action. Hers is not a vague search, but one that begins with the goal of retrieving what's been lost. She works with her situation. This is not surprising if we frame Gold Marie's actions as that archetype at work within the psyche of World Weary Woman that insists she take responsibility. Consciously she seeks what she has lost.

I think here of those World Weary Women who come for analysis, conscious that they've lost their spindle—that which connects them to purposeful life. Having tried to resolve their difficulties with their old industrious attitude of busyness, they find themselves "collapsed at the well," living what feels like a meaningless life. Their first tendency is to want to know what they "should do" to find their lost spindle. They want coping strategies to rid themselves quickly of discomfort. It annoys them that I have no quick answers, methods, candy. Unaccustomed to letting nature have her way, they are unpracticed in trusting the process. World Weary Woman is understandably afraid of letting go of her goals, for up to this point they have been her connection to the outer world.

It is at these junctures, where World Weary Woman has been searching for her way, that the way seems to be seeking her. Not only does help arrive, but it comes in the precise form needed. In Gold Marie's case, it is nature that arrives at the feet of the heroine. She finds that nature needs her. Her willingness to respond with a generous heart brings her the unexpected treasure. This is analogous to that World Weary Woman who gives her all to the requirements of the unconscious. Sometimes, in her eagerness to "get it right," she believes erroneously that doing inner work means abdicating her participation in the outer world. While at first she might resist creative inner life, once its seed takes hold, she might struggle with the belief that this means living only in the inner realms. It is as if in all her years of abandoning the creative spark, once she rediscovers it, she needs to satiate herself with it until she can settle down and trust that it is possible to learn a means of operating with a foot in both worlds, and harmonious simplicity between.

But this does not seem to happen until she learns to trust that her creative life is here to stay. Perhaps she shifts her attitude from outer busyness to inner vocation via daily devotion in picking the ripe apples in the orchard of the unconscious, or "removing its bread" (that is, spiritual nourishment) from the heat of her unconscious emotions so that they are useful as psychic fuel. Perhaps she "keeps house" with her unconscious, working with dream imagery, making its symbols concrete, interacting with what inspires in such a way that the unconscious responds with its riches. On other days, Tar Marie may appear, refusing to do her duty for the soul (or outer world) and the unconscious responds with equal stinginess. We are reminded that nature is two-sided: it has its hellish aspects, as the name "Holle" in German indicates.

Part of World Weary Woman's hellish world is that she believes she must figure out every riddle. Recall that for Gold Marie to develop, she does not have to figure out what to do next. Her assignment, as it were, is delivered by that invisible (if frustrating) higher organizing principle which transcends our own puny attempts to answer mysteries with human logic. Gold Marie did not plan to lose her spindle. Nevertheless, this unexpected turn necessitates a conscious response to the irrational. She moves in the direction of what opens: she moves to redeem what she has lost. Gold Marie embraces possibility, even though this possibility does not come with a map. It is her movement in the direction of the disturbance that brings her to the depths of feminine wisdom, the Great Mother herself.

Willing to move with the unconscious, the archetype as Gold Marie carries the capacity to shift collective consciousness with the gold she gains, for her attitude and heart offer least resistance. She turns from the industrious attitude which has numbed her to her body, and places her feet upon the path of least resistance, even if to do so may be to take a meandering route. On the human level this is easier to understand. We might believe our plan to reach a given goal is best because it is shortest and direct. Yet Fate comes to our door, bringing news, it seems, disruptive of our plan. Ambition pales in comparison to the immediacy and importance of other more pressing matters—say, for example, death of a loved one, or loss of health. All needs reorientation, mobilization around what might restore élan vital.

Ironically, even though the achievement which previously may have seemed so important fades in relevance when sitting at the bedside of an ailing loved one, if grace wills it to be so, psychic incubation on "that other matter" may be happening beneath the ground of consciousness. Through what life serves up, we may be receiving help on that other matter, now relegated to the netherlands of our thinking, as we cull wisdom from experience. The creative process seems to be such for World Weary Woman that what occurs in one area of her heart, cross-fertilizes others, if she gives the experience adequate time, care and space. Having done diligence to the duties of her heart, she may discover treasure that can enrich her other endeavors. What began at first as interruption to her life can turn out to be instrumental in discerning what matters most to her heart, which cannot help but heal.

A Case in Point

I am reminded of this process at work in Esther, who brought to analysis complaints about both her male business partner and her husband. She wanted to divorce the two of them! Her conscious situation seemed clear. If we were to accept her at her word, both situations were quite impossible, the men narcissistic and insensitive to her needs. When I suggested that we wait to find what response her dreams might bring, she turned her anger on me. "Why won't you support me either? Don't you think I know what I need? Don't you support what I feel?" Although Esther holds important positions of central leadership in her community, she describes herself as marginalized in a number of significant relationships where she tries to please, but fails. She has lost track of what pleases her own heart and tends to discount its value. She makes valiant efforts to fit into the mold her husband and partner expect. I suggested that the more crucial thing to discover was how her unconscious responded to her situation.

When Esther returned, her anger had grown. "My dream has nothing whatsoever to say. I need its vote and it pays no attention at all. Instead of showing me what to do, it gives me a ridiculous dream of a garden. What does this have to do with anything?" Gathering courage in hand, I probed: "What was happening in your dream garden?" To which she responded: "Some huge, dark woman told me I needed to weed this stupid garden completely overgrown, gone wild." To the question how she felt about this task Esther said, "I just hate getting my hands and fingernails dirty. That's why I insist my husband or sons do the gardening. I love the flowers but hate the worms so I have someone else do it."

Regrettably or thankfully, the unconscious insists we "get dirty," down on our hands and knees in the soil with the worms. Sometimes nothing can take place to renew life until we place on the compost heap our old, worn-out rigid beliefs about who we are and what we need. In a subsequent dream, the old woman gardener returned and handed Esther a shovel, asking, "Where will you make your road?" The dreamier pointed in a straight line from where she stood to the opposite pole of the garden. The old woman broke into a gale of chuckling. "And there you have it in a nutshell! You kids these days plan your roads all wrong. Look at ours. They are much more interesting. Along them you come to the most unexpected places which won't happen with your straight lines."

Esther's work has been an exercise in increasing surrender to the meandering way which begins with weeding her own psychic garden, extracting all she can from each experience, including the gradual withdrawal of shadow projections.

This leads us back to the meandering path of our fairy tale as it relates to the study of World Weary Woman. Imagine her surprise in finding what Gold Marie discovers, that what she has lost is redeemed in the most lowly place. I am reminded today, on Epiphany Sunday, of that other lowly place several thousand years ago to which the Magi came seeking the new king. The divine child was not to be found in the castle atop the land, where the collective might look. Instead, the Magi found the Christ Child amongst the animals and dirt, hidden in the manger. There being no room at the inn, his parents had to find another atmosphere in which to bring forward the new life and its rarefied consciousness.

And so it is for Gold Marie. There being no room for her in her world without the spindle, she must seek another place in creation—one where few would think to look—down through the well. Her rebirth comes through the round trip into this birth canal connecting her with Great Mother and with her own dual nature.

A parallel is found in the collective story of World Weary Woman. Just as Esther looked last to the dirt for resolution of her worn-out relationships, it has been through fertilizing the soil of her creative imagination that new life has begun to flow through her. Today, when she gets caught in a full-blown animus onslaught, with its outmoded opinions and projections, at times she remembers to return to her knees while tending the needs of her garden. Each time she trusts this new way, Mother Nature cares for her on the individual level, even though it is slow going and fraught with bouts of regression. It is not easy to give up opinions. It is much more comfortable to believe what others have told us than take the trouble to examine the truth of our own personal experience and trust it.

How might this be viewed on the collective level? Again, we can turn to the fairy tale for a hint of what takes place. We might imagine it as the progression of Gold Marie. She realizes it is up to her to go on the adventure of retrieval. As she sinks down into the well, she grows disoriented until she awakens in the depths of creation. Within the collective psyche, we might imagine a newer center of life in a young creative impulse hovering on the threshold of awareness. In its exuberance it may become excessive in its movement, its energy gradient moving it further and further away from its source. Eventually the momentum becomes so great that the impulse loses connection with its ground, and it can function no longer, thus sinking down into the abyss of the unconscious so that it can replenish itself, regenerate. What begins as a seemingly random movement ends up becoming a healing one.

Gold Marie, as far as we can tell, had no notion that her loss would provide the very vehicle for a return to life with gold. What began as suffering became a source of creation's wealth. All these little unexpected surprises along the meandering path seem to prepare Gold Marie for a heroic return where even her stepfamily receives her with a more solicitous attitude. Although we might think that she has been delayed from obtaining her lost spindle, the truth is that each unexpected task to which she responded with a kind heart helped prepare her for her return home, her center, intact. Here is where she encounters the gold she never expected, nor dared to dream: her world responds in a way that enriches her. It is this very outer world onto which once she projected blanket anger that bestows support, to the degree she offers it to herself. She can never again be victimized without her permission.

That is on the archetypal level. How might such an interplay of archetypal forces within the unconscious shine through in the individual? World Weary Women's stories offer numerous examples of such a process at work. Study participants described their thoughts and feelings of impatience and irritation when their ego goals were thwarted. There was some invisible organizing principle against which their protests meant nothing. But retrospectively, by the tenth year of our research, most could find a unifying thread weaving in and out of what seemed, at the time, to be obstacles. Ironically it was the challenge of delay that enriched the journey.

This was my own experience also. As indicated earlier, completion of the study was fraught with unanticipated barriers. Twelve years ago the original idea for the research concerned itself with another topic entirely, that of the meaning of loss of health to women. However, the circumstances of my life led me into what seemed different waters. I abandoned my original ambitious plan, opting to follow the unknown. This culminated in the first study of these women. I did not expect to find what I discovered—rampant loss through their childhood. Believing my work was finished, I put the project away. The furthest thing from my mind was that my psyche would ask me to pick it up again. At times, it seemed that each challenge was unrelated to the thread spun earlier. However, somewhere toward the end of the muddle, it became viscerally clear that what seemed a detour was, in fact, an enrichment of the issue at hand: the redemption of feminine well-being in the face of loss.

Believing at one point that I had completed this study, I crossed the ocean to convene my research committee in Zurich. What I did not expect was a triad of delays. First there was a snowstorm in Midwestern America which delayed my plane to Washington, DC, where I was stopping en route. I wondered whether I'd reach Europe in time for our meeting. Second, although there'd been no inclement weather in Washington, the morning my plane was to depart Dulles Airport, the entire area was hit with ice and snow. Stuck in snarled traffic, I wondered about this fate. Despite delays, I reached European soil. Three days before the group was to meet, the chief advisor had a serious accident on the ice, which delayed the meeting three more months. Such a series of synchronicities gave me pause. What was there to be learned by them?

A scene from "Mother Holle" returned to restore my equilibrium. Gold Marie did not retrieve her spindle directly. Nor was she isolated in the task. What made the retrieval possible was Eros. She related to each challenge with which elemental nature confronted her. In the end, she did not find the spindle by herself, but with the help of Creation, as Mother Holle, who returned to her what was needed when the time was right. Readiness and timing were all.

One of Great Mother's best representatives in my life (Penny, my doctoral dissertation advisor) has a wise saying that has sustained me through arduous delays and unexpected peaks and valleys of challenge. Simply put, Penny's warm words come back home to my body and mind: "Trust the process." Having lost both her husbands to death and raised five children on her own, she knows firsthand the meaning of these words. Gold Marie's journey, World Weary Woman's journey and my own, all proved the wisdom of such counsel.

Trust the process, regardless where the spindle falls. Follow it, despite dark, cold water. Embrace disorientation. Awaken to what is below. Serve with all our heart what meets us. Remove what's baking from the alchemical oven of feelings. Pick the apples that are ripe with feminine wisdom. Clean psyche's house in simple, manageable ways. Shake the feather quilt until inspiration comes back. Assimilate the nourishment of nature. And when it is time to return to the pedestrian world "out there," do so boldly. All that is necessary to stay connected with the Self will be given generously by Creation. Trust the process.

Perhaps the main deterrent to such trust is reflected back through the archetypal presence of Tar Marie, who lurks in the background. It is easy to condemn her, to imagine that she is "out there," and certainly not part of ourselves. But in doing so, we disown our shadow, and thus the riches that come from integrating and assimilating it. It is easy to understand that we might want to escape what comes from the black *nigredo,* Tar Marie's darkness: the unknown, the chthonic, the earthy.

I have been reminded again and again of Tar Marie in this study, especially when tempted to take shortcuts. It is easy to be seduced by self-imposed deadlines which leave too little room for the irrational. It is not easy to take as long as the process requires to birth and raise one's creative baby. First there is the period of psychic dryness and infertility, when nothing soulful takes root. The temptation is to overlook this fact, settling for something that appeals to the mind but not the heart, to reject what body wisdom might suggest. Once something is conceived, weariness comes back in waves. It is easy to slip into inertia, as the animus whispers: "Why bother? You'll only make a mess of it and who will care anyway? Really, this whole thing is not worth the fuss and the paper it's written on! Better to take a nap!"

Such is the underbelly of the feminine, which can hold our Tar Marie with a vengeance. But even this is part of the process in the first trimester of new life. What looks like "doing nothing" may in fact be psychic incubation. Or, such a period could be avoidance of the work at hand.

I recall Marie-Louise von Franz saying that Jung described one of the strongest challenges to our humanity as our penchant for lethargy. Perhaps we can find the truth of this empirical observation, if not in ourselves at first, then at least through the image of Tar Marie. It is easy to prefer the indulgence of those who would cripple us with excess care, myopic to the necessity of autonomy. It is understandable that we prefer the security of the familiar to daring the journey though foreign soil. It is human to hope that another can tell us what to do to find our gold the easy way, with minimum risk. It is hard to stretch ourselves beyond the comfort of our present womb, until necessity demands it. Leah says it:

> I just don't budge unless I have to. It's funny that people see me as a risk-taker. But in my heart of hearts, I know the truth. I'd rather the goodies come to me than the other way around. It's not that I won't work for a goal. I know in some respects, in ways the world can measure, I am a trooper. I play my part. I am responsible But it is the other ways that I'm talking about, the things I know give me pleasure and even make me more serene, like writing or walking along the lake shore, or meditating. Why do I avoid what makes me feel better? I'm good at confessing my sins to my priest or analyst. What I leave out of the confessional box is what makes me happy and whole. I leave out my soul. I want to feel life more deeply. I say I want more joy, happiness, peace. But the truth is I am rarely willing to do what it takes. I get lazy, I make excuses and don't exercise, eat the wrong things, avoid taking time to walk, reflect, work with my dreams or in my garden! I tell myself I'm too busy or too tired.

> It's true, but not true. The reality is, I'm afraid that if I take the risk to do what's in me, I may not like what I find. Or, maybe more scary, what if I like it? What if I like it so much it turns the rest of my life upside down? Before you know it, my anxiety gets so big it's just easier to take a nap or numb out in mindless distractions from duty to my soul. So while it's embarrassing to admit, more times than not, it seems to take some sort of catastrophic event to force me out of my conventional little rut.

Maybe this is why "Mother Holle," as a collective tale, requires both the loss of the spindle and the mean stepmother to activate the journey to transformation. Without them, Gold Marie might still be spinning away her life in wishful thinking. Tar Marie might still be home unmarked by her choice of idleness, and below, the bread might be burning, the fruit of creation left spoiling, inspiration left to stagnate. Like it or not, this tale drives home the point that suffering may redeem what has gone astray. An important aspect of feminine transformation is that the process is one of attending to the ordinary, daily tasks of life with a loving heart. Discipline is needed.

When discipline is wanting, Mother Nature may be harsh. Tar Marie's laziness leads her to try trickery to obtain the priceless treasure (symbol of the Self). As a result, instead of gold, she is marked with pitch. Her exterior reflects her interior stickiness.

World Weary Woman knows this condition of stickiness: the threat of being "found out," of attempting to get the gold too cheaply. Since her gold is reference to none other than the Self, what might this mean in practical terms? World Weary Women all spoke of their disappointment when they found the neglect of their soul could not be repaired quickly, but could take a lifetime of devoted servitude. The saving grace appears to be the increasing awareness that the benefit is worth the struggle.

This does not mean that the temptation to slip back into old slothful ways is gone. Perhaps this is what makes the disciple Peter so endearing. He means to stay awake, to do his best in protecting Jesus in the Garden. His intention is good. But his primitive shadow aspect wins out. Three times he falls asleep, then brutishly cuts off a Roman guard's ear in revenge for his own failure. His Tar Marie has been activated. Still, Peter does his best. After all, he is young. He is human. And, it is his humanness that touches the heart, his darkness that gives him dimension, his struggle that enriches the meaning of our own.

Is it not possible to look at Tar Marie through such a lens? While the fairy tale does not indicate which sister is older, we can assume that Gold Marie is at least psychologically older, for she is first to go out into the world, the first to sever her ties with home. Little Tar Marie has not let go of her mother's apron strings. Let us remember that hers is a poisonous mother. Stepmother corresponds to the Type A woman whose negative animus has done away with her man. Apparently the symbiosis between "younger" daughter (that is, less experienced in her adaptation to the outer world) and mother holds both back in less differentiated form. Maybe the time has not arrived for her until "older" sister returns home with what she's found.

If we can bring more compassion to Tar Marie than she offers herself, perhaps there might be growth toward higher consciousness. Still, let us not be stupid. Until she suffers consciously, her reaction to kindness is apt to bring rejection. On a human level, we are uncomfortable around the savior complex. When World Weary Woman tries to mask her Tar Marie with too much Gold Marie, we sense something false.

On an individual level, this might mean that World Weary Woman treat her little Tar Marie more kindly. Tar Marie represents her unrealized creativity imprisoned in the chthonic darkness of her unconscious, compressed into a space far too limited to come to life. To cultivate a relationship with Tar Marie, World Weary Woman must get her hands dirty. Since she doesn't like to be uncomfortable, Tar Marie nurses grudges and envies her sister who has experienced the outside world as friendly. Tar Marie is afraid of the too-sudden light which her golden sister brings. No wonder she is jealous. She lives in the subterranean territory of World Weary Woman's unconscious, wishing and hoping for the day when she, too, will be liberated, like a prisoner-of-war, to find freedom of expression for her spirit. But when she does emerge, it is in regressive, deceitful ways which bring humiliation. She is not yet ready for the treasure.

Although Tar Marie seems to be the polar opposite to her sister, she too longs to be valued. She is not accomplished, not approved of except by stepmother. Psychologically, she is that part of us that wants consciousness without knowing the correct attitude to achieve it.

The fact is that each sister is the opposite end of the same whole, the same psyche. One aspect stays hidden to the outer world and consciousness. The other ventures forth. Yet each time the fairy tale turns, the polar opposites come together. Out of the reuniting, there is a return to the individual journey. My fantasy is that some day, with sufficient attending, both aspects can operate simultaneously, one foot in each world, creating balance. This hope is based on concrete precedent. One of the most revitalizing elements of World Weary Woman's story turns out to be her discovery that she finds in the world what she brings to the world. If she brings herself as foe, she meets foe in her Self, her cosmos. If she brings friendship, she finds kin. Either way, consciousness falls or rises dependent upon the tiny choices she makes in the moment. This theme is consistent regardless of which version of the fairy tale we read.

Other Versions

Other versions of "Mother Holle" are given in the original Grimm collection in German. The first was from Kassel in 1812. A second from the Schwalm region was collected in 1822. This version describes the two young characters as maidens, but does not indicate that they are sisters. In it, they are compared to Hansel and Gretel, the story including an edible house in the underground world of Frau Holle. A third version from Paderbornish before 1822 matches the previous one, except there is no mention of loss for the stepmother. However, we must recall that the collection comes from an oral tradition, and bits and pieces have been lost. Yet another version, collected in 1802, comes from the Thuringen Region of Germany. Here the heroine is pushed into the well by the ugly, lazy sister.

In each version of the tale, we see behaviors indicating a missing father and benevolent personal mother. The heroine and antagonist seem to reflect these missing elements: they function in distorted ways, unable to live in the world with correct measure. But even more distressing is that without the maternal, their Eros is wounded. This means a problem in feeling. They split off her unconscious feelings, seem to make an alliance with the missing masculine element in the demeaning atmosphere of the distorted feminine. Both young women project their anger onto other females: the mean maiden treating the heroine badly; the stepmother being cruel to her stepdaughter; and the heroine introverting her split-off feelings in such a way that she harms her fingers.

Apparently the story of this father's daughter's transformation requires a negative stepmother figure to force her to grow and find the enduring treasure in her split-off nature. To the Western mind, the mean stepmother may seem unnecessary, an element of psyche to be willed away. But there is something psychologically quite sound in this ancient tale. The heroic element does not set out on its journey to individuation when comfortable. Generally our need to develop comes from challenge, discomfort. Once Gold Marie takes the plunge into growth, the cruelty of stepmother is compensated by the benevolence of Mother Holle, the Great Mother.

"Mother Holle" is a story about relationships. There is the relationship between characters, and the relationship between each character and her circumstances. Where characters grow beyond their previous rigidity, there is reward. What we are not given in the tale, since it presents pure archetypes (what might be called a comparative anatomy of the psyche) is what transpires within each character. We do not overhear a dialogue among the various parts of the psyche. Here we have the father's daughter as the industrious, beautiful orphan who sits by the well and does what a cruel world requires of her. Finally, when there is no other way out, she must leap into the underground—into nature—to find out who she really is.

While much is made of the mythological hero's journey as one of going out into the world, my experience with World Weary Woman is that she has already been there. She has known the highway, the suitcase, the rush, the race. For World Weary Woman, the heroine's task is rather one of coming home. Prodigal daughters have strayed not only from their origins, but from their inner villages. They seek flight, but avoid the soil of soul. Ironically, it is earthly concerns that bring them what they have sought. The form of these concerns seems to matter little, be they loss of health, a loved one, career, financial security. Underneath the loss, contact with Creation has been broken. World Weary Woman suffers the consequences of detachment from what is natural.

Prodigal Daughters

To return to her origins, to find her true identity, is World Weary Woman's greatest underlying issue. Here there is a turning back, not for the sake of regression, but progression. To come to her nature, World Weary Woman begins to ask herself, "To what are you faithful?" In some mysterious way, for many who have felt split, this sort of contemplative question brings forth a sense of destiny. I once heard Mother Teresa say: "Women who feel God's hand upon them know it. They may not know what it is yet that they are called to do. But they know they have a work to do. To this they are obedient." Several years before her death she told her novitiates: "None of us came here to be a number. Those of you who came to be only this, may as well pack up and go home."[24] The obedience to which she referred was not to outer authority, but to what lies within. Such a sense of accepting one's destiny transcends gender.

Jung put it this way in his autobiography:

> From the beginning I had a sense of destiny, as though my life was assigned to me by fate and had to be fulfilled.[25]

> It was obedience which brought me grace, and after that experience I knew what God's grace was. One must be utterly abandoned to God; nothing matters but fulfilling His will. Otherwise all is folly and meaninglessness . . . when I experienced grace, my true responsibility began.[26]

His devotion was to duty imposed from within.

> All my writings may be considered tasks imposed from within; their source was a fateful compulsion. What I wrote were things that assailed me from myself. I permitted the spirit that moved me to speak out. I have never counted upon any strong response, any powerful resonance, to my writings. They represent a compensation for our times, and I have been impelled to say what no one wants to hear. For that reason, and especially at the beginning, I often felt utterly forlorn. I knew that what I said would be unwelcome, for it is difficult for people of our times to accept the counterweight to the conscious world.[27]

Seduction of World Weary Woman

Ironically, World Weary Woman's quest to find what it means to come home to her true self is often catalyzed by the discovery that her affinity for accolades from others seduces her from her destiny. World Weary Woman, as father's daughter, is seduced by authoritarian institutions which, seeing themselves in her reflection, offer her compliments. She is especially vulnerable to this seduction when she is confused and torn. The need to hear compliments takes her further away from herself. They push her in the direction of "doing for others," when she should be taking responsibility for herself. Until this tendency dies, she will stay off course.

Leah described a dream she had had twenty years ago, after her father's

---

[24] Documentary: "Mother Theresa." (Los Angeles: Petrie Productions, 1986)

[25] *Memories, Dreams, Reflections,* p. 48.

[26] Ibid., p. 40.

[27] Ibid., p. 222.

death. In the dream, she was en route to her wedding and saw her father alive and speaking to her in a vibrant, affirming way. He told Leah how well she was doing and how proud he was of her. However, in stopping to hear his appreciation, she missed her own wedding. When she arrived at the church, it was empty. Although she had a difficult time entering her imagination, she felt the need to make contact with him, to discover what her dream was saying. By dialoguing with the father figure in her dream, she engaged in what Jung calls active imagination. In a state of deep relaxation, she heard him "tell" her:

> I am here because you are not believing in yourself, and so I boost your ego with my compliments. This seduces your ego. You are especially vulnerable, exposed when you are confused and torn apart. Remember how I compared you to your grandmother . . . so supportive and loving and kind, like she was? This compliment gets you further away from the Self. The need to hear compliments takes you away from the Self. Compliments push you in the direction of "doing for others," when you should be taking responsibility for your own life. Until this tendency dies, you will stay off-purpose.

Falling into the Victim Role

The stepsister in "Mother Holle" lives in the psyche of World Weary Woman as shadow. Tar Marie is the internal aspect of World Weary Woman. She runs to the goal without relatedness or consciousness of its meaning. Her need for approval can leave her lazy when it comes to attending the requirements of her inner life. As noted above by Leah, despite her accumulation of achievements, when it comes to her own soul the Tar Marie within World Weary Woman tends toward laziness. She must learn to stand up on her own ground. This is possible because her Gold Marie aspect knows about Eros. Until then, her achievement complex continues to be activated at traditional, masculine institutions, including educational ones. Whenever the negative father suddenly takes over, she is thrown into a panic: "I can't understand/do what is required!" This sabotages her.

Underneath is the fear of outshining the father, of going in a direction he might not approve, thus violating the taboo of "good daughter." So her core fear is of the consequences of holding her own independent position: being crucified for it, and losing the intimacy which eludes her. Therefore, her panic around risk-taking masks her ability. She is afraid of turning away from the seductive arms of whatever masculine presence seems to need her—be it an individual, organization or career. These voices affirm her achievements as long as they conform to patriarchal requirements. She feels seen and heard only when she is sought out for advice, comfort.

However, the more World Weary Woman awakens to her own wound, the more she begins to recognize that there is no mutuality of concern. She realizes that she is fueling the outer world's need for support, but there is little reciprocity. She is asked to advise and listen. Her man, mate or boss, attends her needs most when to do so supports his own sense of achievement.

As well, there is an unconscious tendency for World Weary Woman to form partnerships with weak men. Historically she, like her World Weary Man, has lacked real contact with the Self. Since her instincts are foreign to her, unconsciously she attracts similar mates. Together they exert themselves to please the outer world, but leave themselves out of the equation. It is not unusual for World Weary Woman to find herself alone when she'd most like arms around her. That she has needs is hidden by her persona of self-sufficiency. Ironically, she needs, but is reluctant to admit it, fearing that if she gives voice to her need she will be abandoned. In the absence of signs of vulnerability, others perceive her as not needing and preferring it that way.

The Tendency to Oversentimentalize

It is not surprising that World Weary Woman is resentful. But what she often does not see is that in her dependence on men who are absent or weak, she confuses them with her mother. In "Mother Holle," Gold Marie's natural mother is absent. Without a benevolent mothering presence, a child cannot learn from the feminine what is valued or how to relate to feelings of body wisdom. Such an absence weakens the child's groundedness and undermines her confidence. She is left adrift. When she feels ungrounded later in life, and places her trust in partners who appear confident publicly, but suffer uncertainty with their own instinctual guidance, she is headed for trouble.

Part of the problem is that her partners reflect the weakness in her own inner masculine attitude. Such a distorted animus leaves her with many opinions, but too little discernment about what is correct for her based on her own experience, so she becomes vulnerable to victimized situations. World Weary Woman must be careful not to fall into this old complex of feeling unwanted, unworthy: tricks of a harsh negative animus. She must prepare herself to stand on her own.

It was God's decision, or fate, that she would suffer the losses she has. She must not be seduced by sentimentality. It is too easy to be lulled into unconsciousness by wishing. She must stay watchful against fantasies such as how wonderful it would have been if her child had lived to grow older; if her husband hadn't died; if she hadn't lost her job; hadn't lost x or y or z. She must learn not to compare her life as it is with how it could have been. Those "what if's" have nothing to do with reality. If World Weary Woman grew up in an atmosphere of unhappiness, where one parent silently or verbally blamed the other for life unlived, then it is easy to fall victim to a sense of personal impotence/infertility, and settle for goals of the head. Instead of doing the hard work of parenting her own neglected, inner creative children, she can spend hours wishing for greener pastures, better mates, other children.

With a history of carrying the burden of responsibility for a parent's or sibling's or child's unlived life, World Weary Woman can sink into a vicarious depression. The more she differentiates herself, the more she can give up what is not her responsibility, and with it, the grandiosity to believe it should be otherwise. She cannot save anyone outside herself. This is not to say she cannot be useful. But as long as her actions come from an attitude of saving others, she remains aloof, distanced, above it all. Trying to be a saint cuts her off from her humanity. The truth is that she does what she does because it helps herself. Until this is owned, her helpfulness has sticky strings attached, covering her in pitch. She must stay vigilant to avoid such seductions.

A Secret Sense of Failure

The realization that she is estranged from herself is terrible for World Weary Woman, and makes her feel deeply lonely, discouraged. Her lifelong dream of an idealized family unit seems hopeless. Underneath the sadness she feels rage, but does not know how to express it. If her suffering is deep enough, soon thereafter she looks for help. Her latency-aged animus, her capacity to be in the outer world in a healthy way, is split off because she does not know how to express the level of rage she feels. The story she has been telling herself about who she is comes to an end. In its place, she is left with a question mark. Discovering how little she knows about who she was meant to be is a severe blow, and she is ashamed of how little she knows about what matters most.

Losing Her Spindle

In her drive for connection in the outer world, World Weary Woman misappropriates what is holy, commercializing what needs to be developed in a sacred, private way. Paradoxically, although she has had her share of achievements, she may be unaware of her own value. She tends to equate the two, for she is better at attending others' needs over her own. She could benefit from learning to quit meddling in the affairs of others, but this is difficult because she has given them the measuring stick of her own worth. While she may appear confident in the outer world, it is difficult for her to set boundaries. She is afraid that meeting her own needs will estrange her from intimacy. This is because she lacks intimacy with herself.

Perhaps this is why she has so often given her energy to educational institutions, which are based on archetypal father values. More than a few World Weary Women have confided to me that one advantage of the so-called self-help movement has been this: it has supported their belief that they should be able to accomplish anything by figuring out the solution by themselves. The underbelly of this is that they have found another way to flee the closeness they need but are afraid of.

As she comes closer to birthing more intimate contact with her instincts and feelings, she grows afraid. At these times she may retreat into familiar, industrious ways, fearing that a new life will go up in smoke because she cannot trust that she will receive what she needs to mother this unknown aspect of herself. So she throws herself into projects in order not to feel her despair. She gets activated when doubts of her own self-worth come into play. Feeling undervalued by her mother, her Cinderella nature gets busy trying to gather validation and applause from the outer world. Martyrdom is not unknown to her.

A major task for World Weary Woman is to learn to be independent of outer applause. She must know herself as valuable, otherwise this is a burden for others, who are always called to applaud, adore. She must learn to rely on that which is internal, eternal, that which transcends doubt and fear. Until then, she fears that "leaning" will create permanent dependency, leaving her crippled and far too vulnerable. This is what makes it so difficult for her to come for the depth work offered by analytical psychology or other forms of therapy. She is frightened that if she acknowledges her loneliness, she will be somehow entrapped in a sticky web of pitch from which she will never be able to extricate herself. She has not yet experienced that asking for the accompaniment she has never known brings her to the sovereignty she seeks.

Confusion with Mother

Because she has not had experience with her own feminine authority who can be tender and merciful, World Weary Woman may, as noted earlier, unconsciously seek weak men. During times of greatest fear, when she becomes dependent on men who lack connectedness with themselves, she may confuse them with her mother. One of the major consistencies of this research is World Weary Woman's description of her mother as unfulfilled creatively and psycho-spiritually. Their mothers may have been busy with a multiplicity of chores, but seemed somehow thwarted in their own individuation, although the need was rarely verbalized.

The tendency to oversentimentalize her relationships imprisons World Weary Woman until she can stand it no longer and must do something new. If she is fortunate, the sheer pressure pushes her to a leap of faith, teaching her that she can finally take her own stand and doesn't have to be backed up all the time. Ironically, it is addressing her wound in earnest that brings back zest. Until then, she does not know what is and is not hers to carry. Her own identity eludes her. Her numbness may provoke her to carry a partner's negative animus mother, or an institution's. When this happens, she secretly feels inept, an impostor. But underneath this secret hides still another: she fears that when she stands on her own feet, she will outshine her father. A "good" daughter believes she should not do this, especially if he has been frequently absent. When she diminishes herself she may be hoping that this, at last, will seduce him home to her. Her panic masks her true ability.

Leah brought a dream illustrating this. She was shown the ashes of her childhood playhouse which had been destroyed by fire the day the carpenter completed it. Apparently she and her little friends had played with candles and matches which led to the fire. In her dream:

> My elementary school principal was standing by the ashes, and asked me for my school marks. Although I always got A's, my report card could not be found. The principal looked in the files under my married and family name. The files weren't there. He found my credits finally filed under the name I chose for myself—neither under my married nor family name.

Although I do not intend to analyze this dream here, one thing is clear.

Leah was being confronted with how she was hiding herself. When she is on the cusp of some valuable evolution in her development, she becomes terrified that it, too, will "go up in smoke." Her absolution comes each time she can forgive herself for leaving her father's house. Sometimes Leah needs to protect her shininess from being seen because this supports what is unfolding privately. But when this hiding comes from a feeling that she does not have the right to be seen, or fear that what she values will be taken away, then she has work to do on herself.

Leah's pattern is intergenerational, repeated back through her maternal roots from great-grandmother in Norway, to grandmother in Sweden, to mother in the United States Each had a very difficult time leaving their father's expectations. Her dream came during a period when she had to find her voice within situations that infantilized, at work and in her marriage.

Learning To Stand Up for Herself

World Weary Woman can be impatient. Yet she is reluctant to express her anger directly, simply. Instead of keeping her irritation covered, she takes a big step when she expresses her anger and sadness directly. While she may be good at taking care of others, she is not well practiced in listening to and honoring her own feelings

Several months after the above report card dream, Leah dreamt that she was in a bank, needing to obtain funds for a holiday of rest. (This was something she had not done in many years.) In the dream, the teller was so surprised that she wished to withdraw funds for this purpose, that he did not take immediate action, irritating the dreamer. The manager was summoned. He came out of his office, sat down at the table and began to talk to the dreamer about her real work. He told the dreamer that her work began with rest, which was the best investment for her future. After receiving this helpful message from her banker-animus, Leah began in her waking life to learn how to value what she did, while becoming increasingly realistic about the outer world of her father who valued men and women most when they were publicly acclaimed.

And so it is that there may be a teleological function in a missing father for little Gold Marie and Tar Marie, psychic components of World Weary Woman. She has learned ambition in her father's house, from the masculine psyche. Ultimately, her drive leads to a dead end. There, at her own well, her previous belief about who she is must give way. She must dive in to those cold, dark waters of suffering, become conscious of nature and how she must serve her true goals.

Perhaps father has to be gone for World Weary Woman to begin her journey of individuation. Without the comfort of a nurturing feminine presence, her instincts are confused and she is left, like Leah, in ashes, searching for an identity which cannot come from others. Without a healthy internal masculine presence, she cannot discern how to act upon what the Self intends. For though the Self may not be concerned with this world, she must live in it.

5
World Weary Woman's Wound

The Nature of Her Wound Today

World Weary Woman comes into the second half of life with a masculine attitude, having invested heavily in her capacity for high performance. Historically her goals have come from what she thinks is "reasonable," or "possible to achieve," or "should be achieved." Her intellect has structured her actions, molded her self-expression. Her creativity has been made servant to her ambition. She knows she can "produce." Yet, as she ages and her need to make intimate contact with soul deepens, she notices more and more that her outer productions bring less satisfaction. It begins to matter little whether the outer world rewards her efforts. She struggles to come to terms with what is the center of her life. And she struggles with how to live harmoniously with what she finds, despite her fear that she will not like what she finds.

It is a struggle for World Weary Woman to accept that meaningful creation is preceded by chaos. Although it has been important for her to live purposefully in the first half of life, with the requisite adaptations to convention, so that she can discharge her duty to others in the second half, the need to live creatively becomes imperative for her sense of well-being.

Her hardest trial is trusting that she will be granted enough time and enough resources for the task given her. She has impoverished experience with trust. She has seen too many dreams go up in smoke. Too often, when seemingly on the cusp of life's new promise, she has felt the crush of Mother Nature's darker side through unwanted losses and disappointments. Hers has come to be an issue of faith. Can she trust God? Dare she trust the Creator (or whatever name she gives the Almighty) to care for her with tender mercy? And how can she do so when she withholds this same kindness from herself?

Her efforts to treat herself tenderly are embryonic. Consequently, when treated this way, she can be both surprised and skeptical. She is suspicious of the heart. Does she dare reveal hers, trusting whatever comes? Is it wise to trust the irrational? Paradoxically, if she does not, how can she come to terms with the authority of her own feminine wisdom, seeded within the very human, flawed and unpredictable hidden realms of her body?

Finding the thread to her eternal life, her soul, begins with World Weary Woman's reflections on her current life. To what does she give her focus, her vote? What lives at the center of her joy? Has she given over moments to what endures the test of time? Could it be said of her: "This is my daughter, in whom I am well pleased, for she has lived the creative life seeded in her soul from the beginning"?

Each time I meet a World Weary Woman, I am reminded how deep is her wound. Often referred by a World Weary "Sister," she presents a familiar behavior—one seen ten years ago by a number of those in the original study. I remember the story of another encounter.

Some years ago, audiences were crowding into cinemas to see *Close Encounters of the Third Kind,* a Steven Spielberg film about people in crisis. The protagonists found themselves behaving in ways that were baffling. It was as if their conscious minds, corresponding to Leah's Woman Number One, had one goal, yet something within, with an autonomy of its own, pressed them to pursue paths that were irrational. We witness the clash between conventional living and what is true. Both audience and hero/heroines are led along a mysterious path until the fragmentary clues begin to fit together. Before that, we experience a building tension between the protagonists and the outer world. Without the means to make sense of their actions, they pay high prices for following inner urges. Images begin to press for expression in pen, charcoal, paint and soil.

Although the individuals involved do not comprehend why they must render what seems to spill from their unconscious, they are compelled to do so anyway. It is not until the end of the story that we realize that what appeared crazy to the collective was a valid imperative for them. The experience which urged them to take such a plunge came from inner and outer worlds in communication with one another. By trusting their processes, they encountered a higher form of consciousness. But they do not come to this intimacy without first letting go of their outmoded beliefs. For a woman, this means confronting her negative masculine outlook.

There is a similarity between the dilemma of the people in the movie and the conflict which brings a World Weary Woman forward. She tends not to comprehend what urges her to come to therapy. There is a clash, as reflected in Leah's dream reported earlier, with her Woman Number One, who does the talking first. Meanwhile, her shadow, Woman Number Two, waits her turn, less and less patiently. Distress grows. Often she complains that therapy disrupts her work day. Sometimes she grumbles that she must come such a long way to such a remote place (and a farmhouse, at that). The whole affair smacks of opposition. After all, she is a busy woman, short on time. She describes herself as "having people to meet, places to go, things to do." The problem is, she is exhausted.

It is this clash that prompts her to come to see me in what some city-dwellers refer to as "the middle of nowhere." We do not know one another. The rules are few, the way mysterious. She grows impatient. She fidgets, presses forward, has difficulty settling in, readjusts pillows and posture. Her furrowed brow and shallow breathing betray attempts to conceal her suffering. She is in a hurry.

The more she rushes, the more I find my thoughts drifting. Will I, like Redford Williams (who first named the Type A syndrome) need to call an upholsterer to recover and recarpet the trail they have worn beneath this one-sided stance? Another chicken in the roost, scratching around for what she has lost. This time the finding is not quite so fast as she might like.

There is no fast-food line for soul.

Leaning over her papers and calendar, her tapes and pen, she, like Esther, fumbles with her tape recorder. She is terrified of missing a beat, a word, a clue to understanding what is happening to her. She wants to tape her sessions. She does not trust. Despite her efforts, she cannot control what is rising from her depths. The enemy is here. There is no getting around it—this is an unavoidable encounter with her fate. She dare not come off duty. She might forget what's important—what is?

Often her issue shows up as a question of focus. Where should she turn for answers? Who is the authority here? She has an extensive history of going to so-called experts. She has received answers, advice, none of which has sustained her. The opinions of others can become more noise which mutes the voice of her own body wisdom. Reaching for the microphone to capture for posterity, yet again, another voice, she mutters, ". . . so much to manage. Like the guy who has to keep all the plates spinning on poles simultaneously."

I chew on this image for awhile. The Barnum and Bailey Circus comes to mind. The activity she describes is one that entertainers use in magic shows and circuses. It amuses others, generates fans and applause. But applause dies quickly. The spotlight fades and everyone goes home. Alone in the empty circus tent, the hours spent perfecting her act, memorizing her lines, are little comfort for the loneliness she feels. The effort to "keep her act together" leaves her spinning. Despite her best efforts, she is left empty-handed, running in place, grasping for an elusive, intimate treasure she cannot name.

This is the nature of her wound: World Weary Woman's Amazon believes her industry will help her achieve freedom. Instead, she ties herself in knots. Activity is not the key to independence when unconnected to the Self. She spins confusion with her circles of going about the marketplace in search of what is not there.

What breeds autonomy is something else. Until World Weary Woman painfully discovers that her source of wisdom as a woman comes from a place other than intellectual knowledge, she fights for answers in her head. Unconnected to the necessary thread that would lead her to her own true nature, she does not trust her instincts. Her choices in relationships can lead to stormy times. This is particularly so when she chooses partners who are excessively ambitious.

The source of the problem may not be so much in the interpersonal relationship (although its signs and symptoms manifest there), as in the possibility that each Type A woman is unconnected to herself and, therefore, her autonomy. Ungrounded in her own center, she can become silently dependent upon her partner, who appears more independent. But whenever we stray from our own center and become dependent on others for answers that are ours to find, we begin living a life that is not our own. This breeds trouble. Six out of the eight women in the first study were, or had been, in such partnerships. As one put it, "I guess whether we are married or not, we have to learn how to become single."

While it is not within the scope of this study to focus on marital relations between Type A people, the importance of the subject warrants a brief comment. Initially, a Type A woman in therapy tends to focus on her career, an area where her confidence is high. However, as the nature of her wound begins to emerge and her sense of safety grows, it becomes clear that underneath what she may have described as a nearly ideal marriage, she suffers. This is especially true when married to a male counterpart Type A. This seems connected with early experiences of loss, as documented in the literature, although studies do not indicate what is beneath the distress. As the Type A woman shares the nature of her wound, it becomes activated in times of tension.[28] When she is with others who convey impatience, criticism and unfulfilling busyness, her tension grows. Apparently such partners (marital or business) reflect back to her the internal noise that is a by-product of the polar opposites struggling within her.

World Weary Woman's Struggle

We have seen that World Weary Woman identifies her value with what she produces. Literature on Type A females shows that her orientation to the world is masculine. She can be competitive, hard-edged. This was verified in my sessions with World Weary Women. But these contacts also revealed that if she senses safety and warmth, she can soften. Depending upon her attitude, she seems to vacillate between one and the other. Her public persona seems identified with the hard edge, but her private life, when safe, constellates the elusive anima woman, the Hetaira in Toni Wolff's model. However, if she feels what many described as "compressed," "crowded" or "squashed," in order to gain back a sense of who she thinks she is, she moves back into a more competitive Amazon mode. Her self-perception is that she "hardens when afraid." It is interesting that over the last ten years World Weary Woman has come to appreciate her need for her partner to be confident in who he is, so that she can "come off-duty," that is, emerge as a woman composed of different traits.

World Weary Woman is haunted by the Number Two side of herself she has not met. As Willa Cather put it, "It was as if she had an appointment to meet the rest of herself sometime, somewhere."[29] In her push for praise and control, she has neglected a side of her nature, even though she does not know what that is. But she does indicate a desire to articulate updated questions, even if she never finds the answers. She wants to clear out what has become excessive in her life. She wants to simplify. But she fears that if she does, she will edit out what has value and leave in its place what has none. Historically disconnected from her own feminine wisdom, she is

[28] In contrast, those A women who married B's, while they might complain of the partner's "lack of ambition," did find the peacefulness worth the stress. Perhaps those most distressed were the women who began to discover that their essential nature was beyond A or B behavior, but simply connected with nature without the need to achieve or produce, satisfied to "be" without the overdrive that takes them from the moment. When ambition began assuming a less dominant role for the women in the study, they expressed less dissatisfaction.

[29] *The Song of the Lark*, p. 196.

confused. When to leave? When to stay? She is afraid to trust her impulses. She fears her yearnings. Yet she knows that being unaware of how to work with her fear impedes her development. Momentum mounts. Pressure builds. Part of her is trying to be birthed. The other blocks the passageway.

Reaching a place where ambition fails to bring her the connection to a more meaningful life, she gets "hung up" in labor. Her doubts grow huge and she enters her loss complex, with its feeling of terror. Where is she to turn? Where is there help?

One surprising theme in the first phase of this study in 1988, was the emphasis World Weary Women placed on the importance of their friendships, particularly with other women, from whom they drew support and encouragement. In the research literature available at that time, no mention was made of this value. (This is not altogether surprising when we realize that perception of her stress was not inventoried from her point of view.) Even so, the women in this population underscored the importance of this resource to their development.

Since then, there appears to have been a reconstruction of certain friendships. Six out of the Original Eight mentioned this as a source of pain. From their perspective, their losses and fears produced a turning inward, which some of their friends did not understand, or took personally. When World Weary Woman discovered that she had been neglecting an aspect of her nature, she felt a responsibility to focus on redeeming this side of herself. In so doing she encountered aspects of her friends that she had not been aware of before. Friends who could not tolerate a freer expression of feelings from World Weary Woman seemed to drop away.

The more she acknowledged her own rigidity and gave way to a more spontaneous means of self-expression, the more uncomfortable became those who preferred the conventional her—her persona, the mask she showed the world. This brought sadness. As the traditional part of her identity gave way to something fresh, there was a social contraction of her outer world. One of the oft-repeated fears expressed was, "At this rate, will I have any friends left?" She feared change that would leave her at risk. She feared the consequences of integrating those aspects of her personality which had been neglected. Some might refer to these parts under the rubric of "dissociation."

Jung's Concept of Complexes, or "Splinter Psyches"

Jung's early work was influenced by Pierre Janet and others at a time when there was fascination with the issue of what was called dissociation. While they were not investigating World Weary People per se, what was explored serves as important foundation work for this discussion. When identified with the Amazon archetype, World Weary Women have lived the first part of their lives striving toward rationality. The realm of the irrational, where Medial Woman resides with her embodied emotions, intuitions and instincts, has been the soil of certain unexplainable experiences. It is a place where the ambitious woman tends not to venture, unvalued as it is by the collective. Thus viewed, it is an aspect of life which has remained cut off since early Egyptian days when the sun god and worship of Logos became more valued. Such dismissal of the hidden realms of the feminine, however, does not do away with their existence.

Jung and his contemporaries observed this. His doctoral thesis was concerned with the issue as it expressed itself within the mediumistic nature of his young cousin, Helene, a prime example of Wolff's Medial Woman.[30] The concept of dissociative personality was one Jung continued to explore throughout his long and prolific career. His Word Association Experiments demonstrated the reality of autonomous complexes, or "splinter psyches." This was the first documentation of what Freud called repression.

Jung demonstrated that there was something that interfered with conscious intent. This autonomous aspect of the psyche seemed to operate as if it had a will of its own that could thwart the intention of the ego. A person might say one thing, but then, by a means unknown to her, something else might come forth in her behavior. So it appeared that even the healthy individual was composed of more than one personality, indeed a plurality of autonomous personalities, which Jung called complexes.

What differentiates mental health from mental illness seems not so much an issue of number or type of complexes, but whether there is an intact ego—a conscious awareness of who one is in relationship to the world. Whereas the psychotic is unaware of his splitting because he is out of touch with reality, the healthy individual is cognizant of who he is and who he is not. He has sufficient ego strength to observe his own fragmen-

[30] See "On the Psychology and Pathology of So-called Occult Phenomena," *Psychiatric Studies*, CW 1.

tation, and to endure the necessary tension to reclaim what has become split off in the personality. The personality expands to integrate the split.

Part of the process of integration, according to Jung, was the task of finding our connection to our ancestry. One of the tasks on the path to wholeness involves exploring what we've neglected that lives on in the molecular structure of our psyche. The intention is not to romanticize the past. Rather, there may be benefit for World Weary People to reclaim for soul what has been lost along the road to technological development. As the Gnostic Gospel of Thomas puts it: "If you bring forth what is within you, what you bring forth will save you. If you do not bring forth what is within you, what you do not bring forth will destroy you."[31] What needs bringing forth might heal our fragmented condition.

Our ancestors possessed something that World Weary Woman of today has lost on her way to the marketplace. They knew about trust, that change was part of life's cycle, that the force of nature dwarfed their own. They knew to respect what was bigger, and lived in the Mysteries, the Great Spaces between events. They were not afraid to be humbled by what they did not understand, and they honored life in sacred ways. Although unwanted losses happened, they seemed to know instinctually that it was essential to consecrate their acts, to make a compact with Creation. Particularly when they did not comprehend what was happening, they could set aside time and space in which to rededicate themselves to the Great Unknown.

Huddled together in caves, our earliest kin trusted that spring would come again, despite all signs to the contrary. And when spring came, all that seemed barren would bloom, come out of hibernation, stretch its form toward that golden ball of warmth that came up out of the east, and slipped down into the west at the edge of day.

And they trusted something else. They trusted that, despite their smallness, they were needed by the Great One, who could not make the journey across the sky without their prayers and respect. Our ancestors did not have earthly treasure, but they had something else that sustained them—they had meaning. It mattered that they journeyed. It mattered that they learned. It mattered that they were full participants. It mattered that they knew their story, and that they trusted their place in the Great Story.

---

[31] Quoted in Elaine Pagels, *The Gnostic Gospels,* p. 126.

World Weary Woman needs to know that she matters. When it becomes clear that no amount of achievement will ever give her that assurance, she begins to doubt almost everything she has believed. She believed in the power of self-discipline. She believed in the importance of ambitious goals and striving to reach them, believed that with adequate will power she could achieve anything. She believed in happy endings. She believed that no matter what happened, if she just threw herself into her work, if she just worked harder, she could change anything. That is, she believed these things until an unexpected fate brought the unexpected that she could not will away. What then?

What is often overlooked by World Weary Woman, in all her busyness and achievement, is the fact of her depression. Depression can be expressed in an undifferentiated anxiety, so that the person may not seem depressed but creates lots of intensity and drama. The high drama can be very flamboyant. As she gets in touch with her inner world and its richness, she becomes more toned down, less dramatic. The excessiveness is no longer needed to plug the hole within.

When World Weary Woman realizes she is wounded, she wants insights. She is quick to search for understanding, probing into her situation, looking for clues. She is trying to awaken from her industrious, good-girl trance of going for the perpetual "A"—which she has hitherto used to measure her worth.

Her attempt to solve problems is not new. What is new is that she begins to appreciate that her hard-won realizations, even about herself, do not last if they remain above her neck. Insight is no longer enough. A bridge must be made between what she thinks and feels so that her discovery is given body. She must find a way to contain what must be endured if she is to move into living with vitality and joy. Unless she makes her awakening concrete, her realizations slip like sand through a glass, without changing anything. But a competitive atmosphere makes awakening unsafe.

What Hinders Finding the Treasure

The industrious aspect of World Weary Woman knows well the voice of interruption, especially when it comes from within. With such critical inner screams, it is not a simple thing to mother self-expression because early efforts often produce childlike, awkward marks. When one's worth has been based on appearing polished, the beginner's creative expressions are hard to welcome without support. World Weary Woman has not been taught to cherish her creative children, much less nourish them. She becomes discouraged, frustrated, angry with these less-developed aspects of her nature because, like toddlers, they are who they are, not who she wills them to be.

When the heat of this struggle gets too high, she turns away from the cultivation of this unknown self of hers. She neglects and betrays what wants to come to life, turning her back on the gold that could be redeemed from the dung of her loss. Usually, at least until she confronts the futility of such neglect, she regresses. Seduced back into her previous identity, she attaches to her old ways with a vengeance, trying to will her way back into an existence that was less threatening, albeit at the cost of being numb. Outer deadlines become more pressing than inner work; outer creature comforts more desirable than cultivating the soil of her own being. She has not yet won her "license to become," as one retired woman put it. Until she realizes that running away from herself will only worsen her plight, her drama escalates.

What interferes is that she has forgotten about "pulling the bread out of the oven." What could nourish her is destroyed in the fire of her intellect and its drive to succeed. She has forgotten that fire can be constructive or destructive, that others cannot tend our creative fire for us, and that to create from the raw material nature gives us takes time in the kitchen. Such meals won't be rushed; they require a simpler, truer way.

What makes such alchemical cooking, so to speak, difficult for World Weary Woman is that, again, she is a father's daughter. Having had success in adapting to what the outer world expects of her, she has found some degree of material security in the external. Her achievement complex is activated in institutions and organizations of church and state, where the negative father suddenly takes over. This throws her into the panic of needing to produce more perfectly to please father. She knows how to court him, how to dance to his music. In a sense, we might say that she trusts her own masculine attitude more than the kitchen, because she lacks first-hand experience of how nourishing the feminine soup of Eros can be. But this avoidance sabotages her work on the interior. She fears not only failing her authorities, but also surpassing them. At either extreme, she risks the loss of affection. She fears the consequences of standing her own independent ground, for something in her senses she just might be crucified for daring such an act of sovereignty. Instead, she drives herself to pursue that which reflects well upon those she thinks she must please. Simultaneously, she masks her real abilities, even from herself. She is a divided house.

It is ironic that World Weary Woman, however gifted, lives on such tenuous ground. She feels she does not belong. She has not known a full acceptance, that sort of unconditional love which says "yes" to her existence as it is. This means that there is a fear of self-assertion when it comes to feeding her soul. For if you are here on probationary terms, your good behavior is what saves you from the pain of the original rejection coming into consciousness. World Weary Woman says "yes" to continue her stay, to maintain her visa (permit to exist) while occupying foreign soil. "No" is not a word in her vocabulary, because saying it is too dangerous. Instead, she devotes herself to "trying hard," and like the painting in Florence's Baptistery, she ends up like the woman in Hades who has multiple breasts, but no source of nourishment for herself.

Unnecessary activities which keep her preoccupied and away from the devotion to her soul must be clipped away. She is asked to become conscious of the basic relationship between her masculine and feminine natures as she rounds each turn of the spiral.

Fear of Vulnerability

As we have seen, "Mother Holle" is the story of a driven woman who is industrious (that is, good and beautiful by collective standards) but estranged from the well of imagery which leads to the gold of her soul. What gets in World Weary Woman's way is her agenda—the need to know where she is going, when, and what it means. She brings her preconceptions to her ventures into strange territory. She is accustomed to being rational, comfortable with knowns, wary of unknowns, and prefers to lead rather than follow.

Underneath her resistance is fear; entering the journey to undiscovered aspects of her nature can be overwhelming. With a history of times when she felt thrown into chaos without support, she is afraid of being swept into the process of creation. What if she finds herself floundering alone? What if others see her flaws and vulnerability and she is disgraced when such carefully concealed imperfection is revealed? She has not learned as yet that her so-called flaws are her gold. She keeps grace at arm's length. What she does not understand she does not value. Even though this was not her original state, she has been detached from her role in creation, which makes the chaos it brings difficult to endure. Meanwhile, her old way of operating is dying. The need to find meaning from that which seems incomprehensible takes over and leads her into a long forgotten place.

World Weary Woman returns to the development of personality in part when she confronts pride—that sort of arrogance that takes over when she concludes that she must "keep it together," or at least appear that way to others. As long as her energy is invested in persona values, pride continues to divert her life force from healing directions and obstructs growth.

Signals

Thoughts such as these signal vulnerability, which may give rise to the temptation to leap into an achievement persona to escape the discomfort:

"What will people think if they see me raw, naked?"
"Will I be taken advantage of?"
"Will I belong anymore with people who appear to have it together?"
"What if I get stuck here?"
"What if I drown?"
"Won't I let others down who need me if I am taking care of me?"
"I ought to be able to handle this myself!"

Behaviors

Behaviors such as these indicate that one has taken refuge in protection:

Unwillingness to admit that she is suffering and feels out of control.
Unwillingness to admit powerlessness, appeal to larger forces.
The sense that she "should" be doing the process "better" or "faster."
Unending irritability and blaming others for her unhappiness.
Emotional explosions that are out of proportion to the immediate circumstances.

World Weary Woman has faced and resolved past problems through massive efforts to "understand." She has exerted a sort of magical thinking that goes something like this: "If I can understand what is happening, and even better still, why it is happening, I can somehow get myself away from this damnable pain." "Why" is one of World Weary Woman's favorite questions. When needs of the heart have been buried beneath habits of the mind, why's and wherefore's take on enormous power.

What this means is that World Weary Woman tries to figure her way out of tight, unfamiliar, and worse yet, menacing passageways. But this strategy will not work to alleviate her suffering. Each time she attempts to understand what is happening, what might bring redemption escapes her grasp. It is not yet time. She can resist this all she likes. But if the apples are not yet ripe, they are not yet ripe. Seasons cannot be pushed to force the harvest.

So here she sits. She must tend her task, trying mightily to concretize whatever new life is forming outside her awareness, yet with nothing socially redeeming to show for her efforts. Like Maid Maleen, she is trapped in the tower of her thinking, without any way to break through to freedom. Rational thoughts make no dent in the thick walls that imprison her.

The problem is with a distortion in her masculine attitude. The source of the interference comes from trying too hard to be the good girl, the good student, who fears disappointing others. Why is it so terrible if others are disappointed? This seems to be a real American problem. The reality is, sometimes we do disappoint. So what? What is the tragedy? The threat?

Worrying about doing something perfectly destroys relatedness. We are left with "Thou shalts" and "Thou shalt nots," but not life. Resolution lies in going in the direction of life and seeing where it leads.

World Weary Woman is a pro at citing references, embellishing on what is wanted, and, in infinite ways, improving upon what is simple. It has become incumbent upon her to "perfect," to make "profound," to transform the ordinary task into an extraordinary production. Ceaselessly, she looks for the reason, the cause of fault, in herself. She has been taught to do this. She searches for details. But they change nothing. She may even discover, in therapy or education, things which are interesting to her about herself and her origin. But still she is left, like the rest of us, with the task of asking what life there is for her in her present situation.

It is a great struggle for World Weary Woman to accept the ordinary in herself. This, she fears, is not enough. Yet her healing lies in that "one little egg," the trust that she is enough as is. Nowhere do I observe the difficulty of this task more than in the studio, where in hushed tones she whispers her desire to paint, write, sculpt, dance, sing or play an instrument. But, she reports, "Whenever I attempt to express myself this way I feel so incompetent, like a little girl who has never learned the first thing about real creative life." Even those who are masters in one form of creative expression complain of the same frustration when facing a new art form. World Weary Woman has not learned to trust that however she expresses what she feels, it and she are "enough." The fact that her self-expression in one medium or other is primitive has nothing to do with worth. To find the truth of this, she has to let go of her industrious striving for love via what she produces.

The wound that World Weary Woman suffers is that she must produce the extraordinary, that she cannot trust that to be human will ever be enough. Her task is an uphill battle, not unlike that of Sisyphus. Her redemption comes when she unravels that one simple thread which connects her to her humanity, and reconnects her to her own very real firsthand experience of mortality. She no longer needs to be the one who sits atop the world, but joins it, plants her feet on the earth, resigning from her need to excel, in order to have the right to exist without having to be "extra-special."

Added to this is the fact that she may have developed such high-level compensatory skills to mask her feared fatal flaw, that she can become trapped in multiple projects—torn in too many directions. This fragmentation leaves her even more estranged from what she values and what she feels. She is but an empty husk mouthing the opinions of others as if they were her own, for she has lost her original experience and the voice that grows from it.

One of the most difficult tasks of all, then, for World Weary Woman, is for her to sacrifice all the many things that hint of potential. Instead, she must learn to trust what brings her life *today,* however small and imperfect it may be. Although such trust may seem like an indulgence, it is anything but. For World Weary Woman, letting go is the supreme sacrifice. Deep down she fears she will be left empty-handed and empty-hearted, again. Isn't it better to run after many things at once in order to put this fear to rest? Yet deep in her heart she knows that her many achievements have left her empty. In place of a sense of wholeness, she has learned to settle for scraps—little bits and pieces of life that are a hodgepodge. With these she tries to fill the crevices of loneliness.

We need to make our mark, so we can discover how we've been marked, and what our mark can serve. This is tricky business. Because even though by collective standards World Weary Woman has produced industriously, she is poorly practiced in creating what nourishes her from clay, paint, ink, sound, wood, movement, metals, fabric or soil. Especially if what she makes has no discernible outer value.

World Weary Woman's reactions to working with such materials are a reflection of her ambivalence about the creative work she needs to do on herself with the particulars of her life as the raw material. In my practice, this is a time of deep struggle. At first, there are cries of "But I don't have time," "I am not an artist," "I can't draw a straight line," "I am not creative," or "My brother/sister is the creative one in the family, not me."

Despite her protests, something in her longs for whatever will liberate her from this arthritic attitude. I remember one such woman who waited nearly twenty-two weeks before daring to enter my studio, which is next to my consulting room. Later, she confided she felt she wasn't talented or entitled. She felt her "marks" would be too childish.

Of course she, and others like her, have dreams of expressing themselves along original lines. But somehow she comes for healing with an attitude that what is not perfect or already mastered—artistically or psychologically—has no right to exist, much less be expressed. She has the erroneous attitude that she should be able to express herself artistically by virtue of talent, or else she has no business expressing herself at all. What the untaught artist (that is, unpracticed at self-expression) does not know is that "talent" is only one tiny part of artistic endeavor. What separates the artist from the nonartist is that the former knows the necessity of staying at it, unattached to the end-product, despite untold filled canvases, disastrous melodies or manuscripts. Everyone is an artist of some kind, however unpracticed. But until this fact is claimed, "talent" is simply something with which others are "blessed."

Being cut off from her own instinctual nature, World Weary Woman attempts to use another's way to find what she is missing, the treasure that alone can fill the void. Unaware that it resides within, we turn to the outer world, especially in the direction of those who seem to have found their own way. Energy and focus are poured into figuring out what the other did to achieve such an end. What was their method? How can we adopt it for our own? How can we obtain such gifts, with a minimum of pain and effort? Looking for shortcuts prevents us from connecting with what wants redemption from within.

Feeling unwanted is terribly painful. It is replicated again and again when we treat our own creative children the same way. The question is how to offer ourselves as receptive earth to our creative energy, that one flicker that stirs our imagination though we may admit this yearning to no one.

False Mothering and Functional Busyness

Because World Weary Woman has not received the warmth needed for her inner self to thrive, she lacks adequate ground. Not infrequently this is reflected in her language. I am struck with this recurring theme as she recounts times of greatest stress, and does so with mixed metaphors, reflecting the busyness of her thoughts which lead to her exhaustion. (Mixed metaphors are used intentionally in what follows.)

While she might begin to describe her experience as one of "needing to thrive and blossom," she is apt to shift mid-image to another that can leave the listener with the feeling that "this is a bit much." For example, she might shift from a gardening metaphor to a mothering one. She has not experienced a way to nourish her own uniquely creative spirit in a way that brings it to life and sustains it. Feeling cut off, estranged, she seeks to fill this void with mothering the 10,000 babies who are not hers to mother. Rather than nourishing and caring for the "one little egg" that is hers, she turns in whatever direction pulls at her apron strings, because in doing so at least she feels needed. But this is not so much being needed for who she is as for the function she can serve, known only as object rather than human being.

Turning wherever her mind is tugged, she replicates the inner wound. In her refusal to cultivate what is hers, she abandons the new life which grows from her unconscious suffering. Meanwhile, as she continues jumping over hurdles the outer world has set, the sheer busyness keeps her sufficiently exhausted so that she fails at her true task.

What Makes It Hard for World Weary Woman To Create

World Weary Woman's industrious personality seeks peace but cannot find it in traditional or conventional religion. Too much talk, too much of her own noise from too much outer activity, distances her from faith. One World Weary Woman dreams the following:

> I am in a cathedral praying. Suddenly I am interrupted by the sounds of tourists who are chattering away and taking photographs so that flashing bulbs are going off. The tour guide is talking very loudly, unaware that anybody might be there praying. I am very annoyed. I stand up and confront the woman and tell her to take her tourists out of this place im-

> mediately. Then I walk to the back of this holy place and find a red marker waiting for me to make some sort of mark on the stone wall. I write in red pen the following "It is not a weekly affair with God that is needed, but a daily walk."

She says,

> I awaken knowing this is a "red letter" dream. I have no affiliation anymore to any organized church structure. I fall asleep in churches and temples. They are dead as far as I concerned. But in the dream I have a completely different feeling. Here I am content and outsiders interrupt me from what I need.

Looking out the window at what the neighbors think holds us back from attending to who we are. Looking outward pulls us away from discovering what lies within our heart. That rich treasure, in the core, remains within a darkened, silent chamber which never gets visited. The center of our true nature is lost. The outer world seduces us with its promises, all of which tear us away from our own heart's song.

This is not easy stuff to swallow. It is not easy to live the requisite isolation imposed by following our own drummer, as Thoreau counseled. We are, by nature, social creatures. We learn by exchange. But real exchange lies in the dynamic of what is true. This means facing ourselves squarely in an undistorted mirror—a mirror which reflects back to us our own responsibility for our unhappiness. This is not a pretty sight, but when we have the guts to see it clearly, the result is humbling. In the arrogance of our so-called New Age consciousness that preaches we can be anything we want (including that for which we are not intended), and can have anything we crave (including that which brings excess rather than fulfillment), we are led down the dead-end road of believing we are God.

This week, I returned to the well of creative possibility, to the studio. At first I was terrified that nothing would come as I sank into the dark waters of the unknown. What did come was an image of the Woman at the Well. The first time we met in dream-time was forty-eight hours before my son Matt died. In that dream she asked me whether I was ready to surrender to a test which involved painting and writing the original details of my own experience. When we met again she was not alone, but was followed by an endless parade of women from all cultures and all time, each dressed in the same black cloak, gown and cowl. Each had the same gold and silver cross and crescent moon on her forehead, and each chanted a universal song whose language belonged to all women who had suffered this initiation. I awoke knowing that someone I loved was to die, and that experiencing this without flinching was my initiation task. Two days after, this dream image manifested in waking life in numerous forms. I could not change what was happening. The only option was to surrender to something beyond my ability to comprehend in any way that was logical.

I grew to know the well in the years after my son's death. There was a time when the darkness in my heart became so black, when the hole grew so gaping and the pain so great, that it became a well into which I just had to jump—like Gold Marie in "Mother Holle." There was no other place to go after the death of my son and the shattering of my heart.

I was terrified. The water was blacker than ink, colder than ice. At first I splashed and gasped for air, falling, spiraling downward, sure that I would drown. The sounds of my gulping for air echoed in the caverns of my being. I knew that I was breaking apart, drowning, suffocating, and that I had no choice but to enter the experience completely. This was no place for half-way participation. Nor is it, as any World Weary Woman discovers, a place for tourists. This is a place which demands a daily commitment.

It is now ten years since that time. Until this week, I have not been ready to return to the Woman at the Well, to bring her image forward. But in the process one thing became very clear. She is absolutely real. She is real in a way that cannot be comprehended when I operate in ordinary daily life. But despite that, it is this expression of the Creator that is behind the scenes of my life's play, weaving together the strands of my tapestry, responding as she does to the Call and to orders from the Highest of the High. It is the well that is her habitat, her studio.

The Woman at the Well is the keeper of the mystery. She never leaves us. It is we who abandon her each time we ignore our true center. But until our boundaries grow strong enough, until we say "no" to all the many forms of leakage through which other people and outer concerns permeate and displace us, we will never know her, never find her peace, her comfort, her loving arms that patiently await the embrace she longs to give when we are ready to receive.

6
Modern Problem, Ancient Roots

Where might World Weary Woman turn for help? A few years ago I had the gift of meeting one of America's finest African-American writers, Dorothy Randall Gray. Dorothy told a group of colleagues: "If you want to see where you are going, look back, look back, look back!"

What makes the "looking back" she advocates different from that variety of looking back that turned Lot's wife to a pillar of salt? Perhaps what differentiates the two is a certain discernment. Is World Weary Woman's need to look over her shoulder a sign of regret, a desire to sentimentalize the past? Or is her looking back the search for roots? Does she look to the past for escape or for remembrance? Does she turn around to avoid where she is, clinging to fantasies of what might have been? Or does she investigate the past to find context, connection, containment for her current dilemma?

Redemption of World Weary Woman's suffering does not come from continuing to romanticize life, but from accepting the roots that reunite her with Creation. To these she must return, as the thirsty, weary maiden to the well, if she is to find the living waters that alone can heal.

World Weary Woman and the Problem of Our Time

World Weary Woman's fragmentation may be a product of our time. In her attempts to be "liberated" she has settled for a half-man, half-woman mix which is neither one nor the other. She has neither known nor nourished her own womanhood. With a negative mother problem, she has seen herself as being here on provisional terms—and identified as the victim. The more powerless she has felt, the more power she has sought by attempting to "play with the big boys," as one woman put it.

Mary Katherine, or Mary Kate as her friends call her, like other women in this study, does not come from a home where her mother consciously tried to do her harm. Nonetheless, with her parents' preoccupation in other interests, her feelings were neglected. As she grew, she turned toward her father's world. What was missing was experience in the feminine mysteries. She said:

> I feel so behind. I am sixty-four years old. Part of me says "You must be nuts! It's too late. You're not a kid anymore." But the other says, "Shut up! I'm not finished yet. Better late than never," and all those pithy little things. The reality is that I am still here. I am scared. I feel like a little kid that hasn't been to school yet, the real school, that is.

She is ambivalent. One part of her is desperate to discover what is on the other side. But another is terrified. Back and forth she goes, now advancing, then retreating from contact with her depth, from having a dialogue with herself.

Mary Kate feels frustrated when she does not get what she seeks. This is when we see what she calls her "fighting Irish blood." Competitive in masculine ways, at times she becomes what Jung called an anima woman—communicating such a vagueness of identity that she loses touch with who she really is—leaving it to others to project upon her what they will. But when charming and accommodating the masculine world does not bring satisfaction, she can turn vicious with animus judgments, opinions, cutting remarks and impulsive acts that leave her men quivering in fear, willing to do anything to appease her. Or, likely as not, the situation escalates into a full-scale battle: his moody anima at war with her irrational animus. It is then that she wounds herself and others.

Yet it is the wounding that compels her along the passageway in hopes of entering through the closed doors to her own feminine authority. As Mary Kate pointed out in her first glimpses of what was at stake: "Whatever we are told publicly about womanhood is a whole different kettle of fish than I find for myself. Maybe it has to be this way to guard what is inside."

Before she began her journey consciously at sixty-one, following the death of her husband of forty years, Mary Kate strove for something different from a modern-day version of the Eleusinian Mysteries. She was good at playing with the big boys, but she and others, some much younger, have told me that playing with the big boys is or was at the cost of their own big woman. During the analytic process such women have had their attention grabbed through dreams of hemorrhaging, tumors, breast engorgement, starvation, theft, slaughter, drowning, a myriad of health concerns. The Big Woman seems aware of a woman's disdain for her feminine nature, and brings messages in her own way through psyche and matter.

When tension escalates in her interpersonal domain, World Weary

Woman spins fantasies of tomorrow faster and faster—many of which frighten her. She believes industry is the answer to her fear. Recently one such woman shared her anxiety in these words:

> If I don't stay busy in the marketplace, what will happen to us? If I don't do what my boss expects, even though it seems so destructive to my nature, I'll be out of a job. I can't depend on my husband. It doesn't seem to bother him that we can't pay our bills. If I don't take care of our family, no one will. There won't be any help.

She is a prisoner of her own early wound. She replicates it: just as her soul needs were neglected at critical times, she has learned to do likewise. She abstains from pleasure today in her striving for a guaranteed tomorrow. It is a wound whose roots run deep.

An Ancient, Archetypal Problem

Such a struggle is less evident in the Original Eight involved in this study as they have aged. However, I am told that when they feel stressed today, there is a tendency for this old pattern to be reactivated. This is such a common self-disclosure that exploration of its archetypal roots is useful.

The first record of this form of suffering was written in Egyptian hieroglyphs in 2200 BC. The author of "The Dialogue of a World-Weary Man with His Ba" journals his conversation with his soul at a time of misery so desperate that he considers suicide. When we look deeply into his words, and consider the feelings which may have imbued them with such intensity, it is hard to imagine that such a struggle went on two millennia prior to the birth of Jesus.

Apparently the human struggle between opposite poles of existence is ageless. I am indebted to the fine work of Egyptologist Helmuth Jacobsohn for his translation of the original hieroglyphs, and those who preceded him, for a frame of reference in what follows.

For at least 4,000 years, World Weary People have struggled with that sort of helplessness which comes when their ego must contend with its own impotence in controlling matters of soul. This leaves a dilemma. Do they, as Thoreau put it, dare to march to their own drummer? Jacobsohn summarizes the issue in this way:

> A man finds himself out-of-step with his time and for that reason is driven to contemplate suicide. But this is merely the starting point. . . . It is the man who lives far removed from God, who has lost every hold

and support, and who now makes a surprising discovery that . . . no Egyptian had made before him, namely, that the Ba, a man's Soul, is a power to be reckoned with even during this life, a power that man cannot escape by any conscious act of will and cannot entirely grasp by conscious understanding. At first, therefore, man finds himself constantly in rebellion against this power within. It is the tragedy of helplessness, not merely vis-à-vis the outside world but vis-à-vis himself. Such tragedy can never be experienced by a pious and upright man living among unbelievers, but only by someone who himself has been gripped by the terror and despair of Godlessness.[32]

Jacobsohn's interpretation of the Ba is as follows:

In contradistinction to the Ka, which represents the world-creating power of a god or king and the life force in every human being, the Ba stands for an aspect of the soul, connected with the uniqueness of the individual. The Ba is able to separate itself from the world and its polarities. . . . In the Pyramid Text the god-king, after his death, appears in heaven as Ba or Ba-like and unites with the other gods to become the Universal Ba, or the Universal God Atum. . . . In the subsequent literature of the dead—the Coffin Texts and the Book of the Dead this quality extends also to the Ba of the common man. . . . The Ba is thus comparable to the Indian concept of Atman, which is described as "smaller than small, and bigger than big" and which also represents both the innermost center of the individual and . . . the all-embracing Deity.[33]

In Jungian language, we might consider the Ba as analogous to the soul, or perhaps the Self.

Psychologically, the World Weary Person has to come to terms with his own uniqueness, which will not be dismissed by the need to belong to the herd. He is asked to let go a collective identification, and for this he also suffers. Early in the dialogue the author grieves out of his despair and wish for death. Then something unexpected happens: his soul speaks as if autonomous. His Ba opposes his will to die. This must have been a shocking experience for a man whose world believed that such a relationship cannot exist before death and journey to the underworld, and that free will was an impossibility. Nevertheless, the eternal comes to the forefront of his consciousness and his awareness expands:

---

[32] "The Dialogue of a World-Weary Man with His Ba," p. 10.
[33] Ibid., p. 9.

> The Egyptian of the third Millennium BC lived essentially as part of a religious and national group . . . after having severed his ties with relatives and friends on earth, he appears before the judges of the dead, who examine the life he led on earth.[34]

Apparently the intent was to evaluate whether he had achieved the goal of living his life in accord with the collective norms detailed in the Maat, the law. Here there was no room for expression of personal identity. Since such individual feelings were believed to be housed in the heart, it was weighed after death to ascertain a personal truth.

The Ba's role was related to one's heart, one's personal truth. But the individual was not to come to this aspect of himself before death, for this would interrupt his allegiance to living like everyone else, in accord with collective expectations. That something arose within the World Weary Man independently, as if the Ba had an active will of its own, a purpose in its own right, must have brought about unimaginable intensity. In the culture of the time, sin was the equivalent of knowing and expressing free will emanating from the heart.

The hieroglyphs suggest that Ba seems not to concern itself with the fears of World Weary Man. The Egyptian belief was that peace came to a person when he was reunited with his Ba. This brought wholeness. Through death, rebirth came as wholeness. Weariness, in this context, might be thought of as separation from one's heart or soul. In the text, World Weary Man's Ba reminds him that their reunion is inevitable. He tries to convince his soul to approve his sentimentality, his "drift toward death," but his Ba will have none of such notions. His soul does not accept that "goodness" means following the collective attitude toward how to live and die. This is difficult for the man to accept. At this juncture in his development, he wants to cleave to the belief that happiness should come to him through following the collective letter of the law. But even he knows that without union with his soul, he can experience neither redemption nor wholeness.

The hieroglyph seems to be referring to that sort of sentimental living where we go through the motions of doing what others prescribe, without authentically connecting to our own experience. This might be thought of as akin to the rising frequency of depression. But Ba suggests that such

---

[34] Ibid., p. 18.

conformity is the road to greater unhappiness. World Weary Man is told that false attitudes will not work. Ba suggests that the real blasphemy is in living falsely, performing rites mechanically, without heart or meaning. The man is encouraged to relinquish values that have dried up, no longer serving life, and to "go after the beautiful day."

In the "First Parable of the Ba" (lines 68-80), there is an important reference to the worst grief. The parable refers to a lost child, symbolically representative of unrealized possibilities. According to Jacobsohn,

> This symbol [the child] further suggests that the Ba is not referring to deeds left undone in the outer world, but to something different. It is something potential, lying dormant deep within, a still unconscious inner possibility which, in the "night of the storm," would "break in the egg" before it could be born into the world of consciousness.[35]

The Ba may be referring to an endangered psychic possibility that could otherwise be born in the future.

What endangers the fertility which could come about for World Weary Man with his soul? His Ba, through a process of active imagination, suggests that man's relationship to his soul is akin to the relationship of a man to his spouse. If his heart is hardened, he cannot receive wisdom or gifts from the feminine. This keeps him separated from that part of himself, his anima. Unwilling to accept what is foreign, he clings to his misunderstanding, which isolates him further. His hardened heart, born of arrogance, keeps him walled off from what might redeem his wound. Separated from his soul, he cannot reach for self-realization.

I am reminded of that body of literature which has appeared over the last two decades on marriage between different types of people. The most difficult match seems to be between the so-called Type A man and woman. It is not difficult to see why, in the context of what this dialogue brings to light. Perhaps the weariness of the industrious couple keeps them estranged from opening compassionate hearts to one another. How can we soften our hearts to our partner if we do not do so with ourselves? It is not surprising that participant after participant in my ten-year study described intense loneliness during periods of greatest estrangement from her Ba.

Such a condition has roots. Again we turn to the Jacobsohn's description of World Weary Man:

---

[35] Ibid., p. 31.

> [He] suffers from his agonizing loneliness. He feels lost at a time when justice, wisdom, and religious awe no longer mean anything. He suffers most from a natural relatedness, a rapport between people. A man "with a quiet heart," a confidant, is nowhere to be found. Nobody wants or is able to listen to him—just as he himself was previously unable to listen to his Ba. Possibly he was turned away when he tried as a "wise man" to bring one of the rulers of his time to his senses. . . . He must have had wider and deeper life-experiences than most, and he suffered the frustration of being able to see further than his fellow men without being able to do anything about it.[36]

Such a loneliness is expressed in many fairy tales and myths. The eternal struggle to find a loving atmosphere for one's heart in times of cruel inhospitability is described through stories that endure. The theme is enacted through conflicts that leave both mortals and gods feeling rejected. The issue of feeling unwelcome in one's world is a motif that is part of the weariness of our earliest kin.

Later in the dialogue we come to know that World Weary Man feels homesick and lost from God. But this is a different despair from his earlier grief. Here he is not quibbling with the details of arranging his actions to fit what others would have him do. Instead, he pours out his suffering to his Ba, as if it were a best friend, an inner companion. He communicates his suffering without blame. This is possible because, without being driven by the need for power, he can open to wiser ways. He comes into awareness of what Jung called his "ethical duty"— attending to the requirements of his own soul.

When World Weary Man ceases fighting his soul, he finds that his Ba has a purpose for his life, regardless of any choice this man has made. If the latter cleaves to his longing for death, seeing peaceful union (that is, home) available only in the Beyond, then his Ba will meet him there. But, if he chooses to embrace life in the present, then his soul will be with him in the Now, his grief redeemed. Either way, World Weary Man will be reconciled with his soul, sooner or later. The merging of matter with the eternal, and the enduring with matter, is the Ba's goal. Through the process of this self-realization, personality transforms.

In World Weary Man's dialogue, we find a recorded journey of creative transformation. The author's frustrated search for power brings him to the

---

[36] Ibid., p. 40.

brink. His will power does not bring what he wants, any more than the outer world provides him with what holds eternal value. His transformation comes about through discovering he must surrender his desire for power and instead seek reconciliation with his Ba. He does this by accepting his suffering, finding it to be friend, not foe. It is his Ba which guides him through his transformation. But it is far from easy going. He resists taking such a plunge. After all, how can he trust what is so foreign to his way of living, to his relationship to himself in his world? How can he heed what defies the way of his family, friends, countrymen? How can he go on a journey which is considered the ultimate blasphemy of his times—that of relying upon interior wisdom?

Not surprisingly, World Weary Man begins his conversation with his soul from a perspective of mistrust, resistance and narrowed consciousness. Egyptians did not concern themselves with security or happiness in this lifetime. Their focus was on the Afterlife. If there was transformation to be had, it was after death. As years passed and the sun god (Ra) became dominant around the middle time-span of the old Egyptian Kingdom, writing, mathematics and the arts were born. Human beings had a means of expressing relationships. That was when a split occurred between the rational and the irrational. The irrational, or feminine, aspect of nature in humankind was repressed. Affects and impulses were considered less valuable and relegated to the underground, associated with suffering. Marie-Louise von Franz succinctly describes what happened:

> Part of the primitive individuality of the Egyptian went into the unconscious [and] . . . . with it went a certain aspect of affect in the feeling life. This aspect of the Egyptian's communal life was concentrated in the archetypal image of the god Osiris. . . . He represented the passive, suffering aspect of nature and the psyche. . . . that which does not move, and which does not have its own volition, which is the greatest suffering on this earth. . . . In the Osiris part of his nature was also hidden the Egyptian's true consciousness of his own individuality, in contrast to the collective ruling principle of consciousness. So the body was associated with Osiris and the idea of the Ba-Soul.[37]

His was an individuality hidden from him until the afterlife. World Weary Woman might relate. Part of her nature which brings consciousness

---

[37] *Alchemical Active Imagination,* pp. 3f.

of her own individuality remains hidden from her. In her ambition, she leaves her body wisdom buried, she often tells herself, until she can "just finish this next achievement . . " Then, she will listen, heed, hold, rest. Or so she says. But of course it does not happen.

As World Weary Man begins to deepen his self-realization, he surrenders to his Ba what is his soul's. His respect and reverence grows. But this takes devotion to his process, and work and time. Meanwhile, his Ba shifts its manner of expression. The Ba seems mercurial in nature, expressing itself in whatever costume and language necessary for World Weary Man to receive its hints. Fighting gives way to partnership.

This is remarkable when we consider the historical context. Never before had Egyptians experienced a collective separation from the eternal, from God. Until then, individuality as we know it was unknown. Instead, the focus was one of conventional worship and building one's life so that reward could come after death. But, as in all cultures, once the spirit of the law (the Maat) was replaced by the letter of the law, then hopelessness, frustration and desperation grew. Jacobsohn reminds us:

> [For] the first time man was face to face with himself and experienced himself as an individual. This must have been intolerable to an Egyptian accustomed to a collective; and it must have been to some extent responsible for the high incidence of suicide at that period.[38]

Somehow World Weary Man was able to endure his impossible struggle in such a way that a new path was forged. As his contact with his Ba deepened, suicide was no longer an answer for him. At first, only the prospect of redemption in the Afterlife brought him reprieve. But with devotion to his process of connecting to the sacred, another possibility emerged. In holding fast to opposite desires that could not be "solved" in one-sided ways, a third path opened. Psychologically speaking, this transcended way brought forth a new center within him that carried the potentiality of wholeness. This is nothing short of a fundamental shift in one's psychological center of gravity.

I am reminded here of Jung's wisdom regarding the process of assisted individuation. Fundamentally, circumstances for the analysand may stay the same. However, because she shifts her attitude toward the Self, and hence, her world, everything changes.

---

[38] "The Dialogue of a World-Weary Man with His Ba," p. 50.

A Modern Need for Dialogue with Ba

World Weary Women interviewed ten years ago expressed similar needs for an inner dialogue. Each observed the one-sidedness of her life. Each had come to a place in her life where she was seeking relief from stress of some sort. As a population, World Weary Woman believed that a stress-free life was not only possible but desirable. According to them, stress would be gone if they could "do it right." They interpreted their conflicts as doing something wrong, or having had something wrong done to them. Their concern was on how to "follow the rules" that would insure happiness. Most of their focus was on what they were doing, or not doing, that might secure a conflict-free future. Those who had sought help concerning their distress said they wanted to be healed of conflict.

Over the past ten years, many of these women have had an attitudinal shift regarding the presence of conflict in their lives, especially the seven oldest women in the study. These women reached an appreciation of conflict as a natural part of life. No longer so preoccupied with the need for cure, they now respond differently to their areas of tension. Each of the women now focuses less on what she does in a day and more on how she lives. She has begun to call into question the role of catastrophe, suspecting that its drama is needed less to justify her right to live, than to live each day as if it were her last, as if death were looking over her shoulder.

While this might sound morbid, the effect of what these women radiate is quite different. To a greater or lesser degree, each seems liberated to enjoy new beginnings as well as to savor completion. More accepting of what she has lost, she is more open, more at peace, with gratitude for what she has found when least expecting anything. What animates her most is the discussion of what she is discovering about what makes her unique. At the same time, she is less competitive in the outer world, more in dialogue with the inner. But perhaps this seed was taking hold at the onset or before the study, in that the participants self-selected themselves for the research. For their own reasons, it was important for them to tell their stories.

Without a record of who she was a decade ago, it would be difficult to ascertain who she is becoming. We need a frame of reference from which to compare individuals within a population, and aspects of the individual within themselves. Without an industrious character, how can we know idleness? Without the Amazon, which is impersonally related, how can we know the Hetaira or Mother, which are personally related? Perhaps this is one function of opposites within the personality. When polar opposites confront one another, as they did in the psyche of World Weary Man, a third aspect is born, a transcendent function which could mediate such a split. This is necessary for the development of personality.

Like the early Egyptian of the Middle Kingdom, World Weary Woman has placed greater value on the solar god known to the former as Ra, with his need for rules and order. Meanwhile her Osiris, that affect which does not have its own volition, suffers in the underground. It is in the body of this suffering that her uniqueness lives. It is in dialogue with her body that she meets the wisdom of her Ba soul. While for World Weary Man of ancient Egypt the Ba soul was to be met after life, World Weary Woman's redemption necessitates this reunion of mind-body (Ra-Osiris) in the present. In the first half of life, she has done what she can to follow the outer world's rules. But her contribution ceases if she cannot meet her own needs, her inner rules. Her task is to bring her unique consciousness back through the development of personality, which can only happen through reconnection with her body wisdom via her struggle in the underground.

Like World Weary Man, she struggles when attempting to find her own individuality, for she fears this will violate the collectives outside and within. She seeks dialogue with the essential core of her individuality until that which is eternal, the *élan vital* that animates her body and psyche (for they are one), is met. She must soak in the Godhead, her well of living waters, reconnecting with the eternal while firmly grounded in the present.

This means that World Weary Woman is challenged to relinquish attachment to Chronos time and enter Kairos. Von Franz once told me that Kairos time is the realm of trusting there is a "right moment," and when we trust the present contact with what's real, the right moment brings unexpected yet meaningful gifts.[39] Over the last ten years World Weary Women in the study have become increasingly conscious of their wounded creative hands and they have yearned to redeem this pain. With each rotation of her spiral-like journey, World Weary Woman converts what is raw into what is usable. In so doing, she discovers something new about her nature. As one sixty-four-year-old woman put it:

> Ten years ago I was concerned about my business. That was my religion. The profit I made or didn't make drove me. What I wanted drove me. What

[39] Personal communication.

> I feared drove me. The fears of the business, and my guilt about not being with my kids as much as I wanted, drove me. But now it is different. I get tired more easily. I can't push myself like I did. I have never been a person to take naps. Now in the middle of the day sometimes I just have to lie down. I have discovered that what I care most about is living with a better heart. I care about who I love and how I love. I care about my garden. Who would have believed it? Now that my husband is gone, I realize how important it is for me to be here. Life is my new religion.

Who this World Weary Woman is becoming seems strongly affected by her history of industry. Having been so busy, her appreciation of idleness at this time in her life is enhanced as she considers new adaptations of her creativity. Peri- and post-menopausal women, who have defined part of their value through childbirth and child rearing, are challenged now to make a leap of imagination into other ways of birthing new life. The issue is no longer having actual children or not. Rather, what grips her most is what creative children are trying to make their way into life through her.

Now, each is forced into new ways of uniting with her creative source. Her dilemma might be compared with the struggle of the artist. In the studio she must find innovative ways of bringing together light and dark, negative and positive space. Each stroke compels her to the next until she completes the work, only to begin another canvas, connected or not to the last. We join Aaron Copland in asking, why must the artist begin anew?

> The serious composer who thinks about his art will sooner or later have occasion to ask himself: "Why is it so important to my own psyche that I compose music? What makes it seem so absolutely necessary, so that every other daily activity, by comparison, is of lesser significance? And why is the creative impulse never satisfied; why must one always begin anew?" To the first question . . . the need to create . . . the answer is always the same—self-expression; the basic need to make evident one's deepest feelings about life. But why is the job never done? Why must one always begin again? The reason for the compulsion to renewed creativity, it seems to me, is that each added work brings with it an element of self-discovery. I must create in order to know myself, and since self-knowledge is a never-ending search, each new work is only a part-answer to the question "Who am I?" and brings with it the need to go on to other and different part-answers.[40]

---

[40] *Music and Imagination,* pp. 40f.

World Weary Woman, like the artist, struggles between industry and idleness, asking and re-asking her soul creative questions. With each rotation of life's wheel, she discovers an aspect of her personality that hitherto lay dormant. It is this process of creative evolution that helps her bring forth what is within, to know this aspect of her nature for the first time. She must honor the creative thread she's been given because it is her connection to the Self. She must find renewed connection if she is to meet this mysterious Self at her center. This is her most essential intimacy—the discovery of who she is in relation to Creation.

Knowing World Weary Woman brings me to wonder whether the genesis of the arts does not begin afresh each time someone picks up a paintbrush, pencil or lump of clay, or sits down on a piano bench or at their instrument, whatever it be. Into the inner culture they go. As if by listening to the gods and the timelessness of soul, in contact and connection with that nameless something which is the source of life, vitality is birthed once more. The arts lead us to the meaning of living. What is important is what is met. It matters little whether what is met is good or bad. Just as it matters little whether my mother was good or bad, my father absent or present. What counts is what I do with whatever is experienced or lost, be it joy or suffering. Am I willing to be a good enough mother to whatever this is? Am I willing to father in a kindly way this hitherto unknown nature that is my own?

As Jung explained:

> The patient can make himself creatively independent through this method. . . . He is no longer dependent on his dreams or on his doctor's knowledge; instead, by painting himself he gives shape to himself. For what he paints are active fantasies—that which is active within him. And that which is active within is himself, but no longer in the guise of his previous error, when he mistook the personal ego for the self; it is himself in a new and hitherto alien sense, for his ego now appears as the object of that which works within him. In countless pictures he strives to catch this interior agent, only to discover in the end that it is eternally unknown and alien, the hidden foundation of psychic life.[41]

Feeling is what leads Weary Ones back to their center. So it is feeling that must be trusted and followed, lest the language of the secret place be

---

[41] "The Aims of Psychotherapy," *The Practice of Psychotherapy,* CW 16, par. 106.

lost beneath layers and layers of trying too hard to explain what cannot be explained, much less fully known. Descartes observed, "I think, therefore I am." One who feels compelled to express his or her own experience might say: "I create, therefore I am."

7
Conclusion: Growth As Process

World Weary Woman is sufficiently defended to require a high intensity of experience in order that her alexithymia is penetrated, and she can feel the enormity and depth of her soul and its neglect. It is then that the other aspect of her nature is apprehended—this hidden part of her unconscious personality. This Woman Number Two, as Leah named her, who has been neglected in the waiting room of her psyche, screams, "What about me!?" Not until World Weary Woman allows herself to feel her rage at her self-neglect does she plummet to the depths of her hidden sadness. Therein she finds the gold.

One analysand who brought a dream initially tried to grasp its meaning intellectually. Her frustration mounted with each protest.

> But what am I supposed to do? I'm coming to analysis. I'm writing down my dreams. I'm paying all this money. I'm spending the time this takes. Meanwhile, my relationships are suffering. I'm neglecting deadlines at work. And what for? To be told by my dream that I'm still leaving myself out? I don't understand. What more can I do?

And this is just the point. With her overly developed masculine attitude, when World Weary Woman has a problem her knee-jerk reaction is to jump into doing, fixing. With an absent father complex, her masculine side is distorted. She holds tenaciously to the structure that action provides, as if it were a lifeline through her present chaos. The more frightened she is, the more she does. Without a healthy masculine model, she has not internalized a means to measure excessive activity. Until she does this, she remains enraged that she must pay with her time and wallet. What makes her angry is that she can't have it all, that she must choose, must sacrifice. If she chooses individuation, she is required to invest a great deal of energy to learn her own symbolic language

Meanwhile, she is caught up in a pseudo androgyny, neither fully male nor female, rummaging about the marketplace for intellectual answers to what are anything but logical problems, until her suffering reaches a level she can no longer deny. Here World Weary Woman begins to awaken to her primary issue: She is cut off from her identity, her womanhood, and without access to its instinctual knowing, she remains disconnected from her body and what her body wisdom feels. She is left spinning in an isolated way, and hurting.

This is not to say that World Weary Woman is exiled forever from the feminine and its redemption through Mother Nature. Repeatedly and spontaneously, the participants in this study alluded to the healing function of nature in their lives. As World Weary Woman matures, she finds herself attracted to nature and its creative mysteries, as she was as a little girl. When she crosses the threshold into nature's domain, she finds herself amazed that mental bustling dissipates and body sensations emerge, leading slowly to the evolution of her own feeling consciousness. Maria Theresa put it thus:

> Ten years ago I was so busy that I didn't even know I was driven or stressed. Like my mother's tranquilized fire, my feelings were numb. . . . More and more my walks along the water have become a place where I find peace . . . a place I can feel and realize that my fire had nearly gone out.

Such a reunion with the feminine is essential to World Weary Woman. Often the reconnection with feelings comes about with increasing time in nature. Here, she discovers both *that* she feels and *what* she feels. Memories of her personal mother and mothering figures return. While World Weary Woman's mother was sometimes described as "trying hard to do her best under the circumstances," she was also reported to be "depressed, unwilling to play, serious, stifled, frustrated, lonely, at times in reverie that no one understood or noticed." Memories of mother's hearty laughter were dim or missing.

Consequently, when World Weary Woman encounters a female model who enjoys life in the moment, who listens deeply and openly and can express caring and nurture for body and soul, she is amazed. The forms and timing of these encounters were varied. As children, some found contact with their feminine nourishment in household maids, cooks, baby sitters; others in school teachers, physical therapists, nurses, counselors, art teachers and art therapists, neighbors, aunts, grandmothers or mothers' friends. But as many grew older, their quest for accomplishment drew them away from such quiet reprieves, onto roads among competitive men and women. As World Weary Woman scurried between positions of power, she moved further from any ability to trust her inner nature. Eventually, she found herself so cut off from her feelings and instincts that it became surprising to find feminine support, regardless whether it was offered by men or women. Anna, the woman who was told in a dream that "gold watches come in many forms,"[42] shared her insight:

> Maybe I'm so surprised to find a woman truly trustworthy because so much of my life I've been so competitive and more available to men than women. I know more what men want from me. They want me to perform, to sparkle, to flatter them like an understudy. But women don't seem to need me as an extension of their own ego the way men do. I know how to play Pygmalion. But when there's no male puppeteer, no strings, that's real freedom, and also, real scary. What do I do with the space? I want it and fear it.

Overall, the story of World Weary Woman illustrates that growth is a process. Conditioned to an attitude that her value is determined by magnitude, her efforts in the past have focused upon large leaps, doing only those things which appear grand. For her to reframe the development of personality as a process which comes about through natural, individual steps is critical. Slowly she discovers that weariness is not her enemy but her advocate. Through bringing consciousness to her condition, she learns to slow down, attend to the natural rhythm of her soul.

Gradually the shift reconstructs her attitude toward herself and her world. As we have seen, the progression of this movement seems to parallel Gold Marie's development in "Mother Holle." It is true that fairy tales should not be taken as personal stories, but rather as narratives from the collective. But as such, each of the characters conveys an archetypal element at work within the psyche. And there are parallels between "Mother Holle" as a tale of feminine transformation and the transformation of World Weary Woman.

As in "Mother Holle," World Weary Woman's story has a missing masculine element. Even when her father lived in the home, his positive presence was lacking in two chief ways: 1) He failed to confront inappropriate behaviors in his wife which were wounding to their daughter; and 2) he failed to support the sexual sovereignty of his daughter, thus leaving her to spin industriously on the highway of life without reverence for her female nature.

---

[42] See above, p. 22.

Without a positive masculine presence to affirm her life in the outer world, and without a benevolent feminine element in the home as a girl, World Weary Woman was left without the means to connect to her feminine nature, its value and instinctual knowing. Estranged from herself, she split off into the shadows any apparent signs of laziness, compensating her estrangement by an overly zealous need to perform, achieve, to please Father. Without an available, emotionally consistent mother or father, she overidealized the masculine world, abandoning her own needs. Instead, she produced what she thought would please others and ended up disappointing herself. The more empty World Weary Woman felt, the more driven her industry. She looked for the right thing (Eros), but in all the wrong places (power). Her story of transformation begins following loss.

In "Mother Holle," we see the maiden, in her despair, turning to the very two aspects of psyche which most reject her. In these two creatures, we find harsh judgment, cruelty and opinions analogous on the personal level to the negative animus. Only after her regressive attempts fail to find support where it does not exist does the maiden face her suffering fully, and the tale progresses as she calls upon previously uncharted depths by descending into her own well of life.

Such a shift is reflected in World Weary Woman's story. She tells of times when, despite misgivings, she turned for help to those very persons who had been cruel in the past. However, without a Good Mother, the feeling tone of the home fails to revere instinctual guidance. Such a child in such a home turns over her authority to the critical negative animus, who crushes new life. Her hypersensitivity to outer criticism betrays an inner insensitivity to the harm she does to herself by auto-aggressive thoughts. Each new bout of outer rejection reflects the inner rejection World Weary Woman heaps upon herself. She describes mental self-chatter in harsh tones: "You are so stupid! Why don't you ever learn? What's the matter with you?"

When she awakens to the fact that help is not forthcoming from abusive internal and external quarters, she moves forward. Recently Esther, trapped in a loveless marriage, exclaimed:

> I cannot go on this way. How did I get myself into such a cage? I've been scared to leave it, but it's worse to stay, too suffocating. I am too drained. I'm not leaving him. It's more like I have to find me. I wish Morrie and I could help each other this way, but he can only see me as his

> mother. I am sad. But it's not my usual depression. For what it's worth, I know what the sadness is.

Paradoxically, progress begins with what feels regressive: a collapse. Like Gold Marie, World Weary Woman collapses in despair before she enters the underground of her psyche, where help is given. Once she accepts the depths of her despair, she is free to reclaim her rightful relation to nature. For World Weary Woman, such a leap seems precipitated by feeling the profound loss of that vital thread which has given her life meaning. Like Gold Marie, she loses her psychic shuttle, that is, the creative thread which links her to her world.

In both fairy tale and interviews, the heroine finds herself moving through periods of disorientation, and new tasks imposed by nature. To the degree that she responds with an attitude of serving intimately what transcends her ego, her soul is nourished. Yet neither story ends here. Despite the nourishment which comes from connecting with a creative interior life, neither World Weary Woman nor maiden can remain in this state without a foot in the outer world. To be true to the feminine nature she discovers within, she must respond to ongoing outer demands, concretizing her feminine way. Making manifest her inner nature in the outer world is part of World Weary Woman's process of coming home.

Initially I thought of World Weary Woman's loss as the crucial issue. But through our ten-year exploration, I have learned that it is her profound sacred suffering that is the raw material of personality transformation.

Over time, following her process, World Weary Woman learns to consecrate what is created through her life. This begins by making room for resting places. Her task is to rest what is weary, to activate what has grown idle.

From my first meetings with World Weary Woman, it was clear that she could work. She could analyze, psychologize. But she had not learned how to play. This again brings up the importance of the pause—in the smallest sense, of a few minutes in an otherwise busy day; in the larger sense, of the analyst's office, or confessional, or studio as a pausing place. Pauses in time and space are needed to connect with those instincts which have to do with enjoying life from the neck down as well as up. It is in pausing to connect with her own inner wisdom that World Weary Woman learns to create, not to achieve but to engage her whole being, to cultivate what brings joy, to savor her connection with the cosmos.

Thus she transforms her suffering through a sacred return to creative living. Esther recently put it this way:

> I just couldn't figure out what was draining me so much. Now I realize that when I feel so tired, it is because I'm not growing. But when I'm in safe places, supportive, fun and creative, I'm happy, alive, looser! I need not only community, but creative community.

Softening those aspects of personality that have stiffened gives weightier form to those which have been too ethereal, abstract, heady. Little by little, World Weary Woman discovers that living vibrantly is a creative process, an intimate experience whereby she becomes fully known. As she finds her intimate tap root, each day is an exercise in active receptivity to what she did not anticipate. The intuitive must cease her wild plunging about, the thinker must learn to trust feeling. Movement is slow, often painfully so. Her internal shadow sister is seduced time and again by the hope of shortcuts. But cheap tricks fail to provide what she needs and yearns to create.

Yet, even here, one has the impression that as World Weary Woman discovers her own darkness and laziness regarding duty to her soul, possibilities dawn for growth. When she surrenders to the self-regulating tendency of her psyche, a gradual shift takes place, even if barely perceptible to the outer eye. With the emergence of each new challenge, the development of her personality seems to require a rotation around the Self. Such a movement follows a particular progression.

We have noticed that when World Weary Woman's loss complex is activated, she reacts initially with the Logos characteristic of the Amazon. She gets busy. She asserts her independence. She operates solo. She becomes excessively industrious. Increasingly exhausted and frustrated as her attempts are futile in producing the peace for which she yearns, she moves unconsciously in the direction of Mother. Weary of worldly ways, she is drawn to safe hearths, by which she can warm herself. As a connection builds between her Amazon and nourishing Mother, the inner struggle finds a deeper containment. Within such an inner and outer milieu of safety, a place where she is released from the demand to achieve and the pain of criticism, she is free to explore what suits her. And what suits her most is following the trajectory which fosters the eternal within. She gravitates to symbolic realms, the domain of Medial Woman. Crossing over the borderlands into Medial Woman's domain, World Weary Woman finds herself fascinated by a growing intimacy with the symbolic life. Previously unaware of guidance available through her body, dreams and creative expressions, it is as if she discovers the real curriculum.

But dwelling permanently in these underground places is not her fate. Just as Gold Marie grows homesick and must return, so too does World Weary Woman. Sooner or later, she feels her own form of call and must respond. Again, she moves on toward the terrain of interpersonal relatedness. In "Mother Holle," the maiden returns to the home of her stepmother and lazy stepsister. World Weary Woman returns to her outer world with deeper awareness of the importance of intimacy. This brings her to her inner Hetaira, who longs for closeness and union instead of the emotional distance she has hitherto experienced.

As this is the least developed and affirmed aspect of her nature, World Weary Woman can fall victim to feelings of inadequacy as lover. In the past, her inner stepmother-stepsister chatter has mocked her desires and dreams for intimacy. Yet her need for passion is real, even if she feels frightened, vulnerable. Perhaps, in part, this has been factored into the pattern of her personality's progression. Leading from safest places in her psyche first, she prepares to greet the unfamiliar in herself, step by step.

Summary

The dynamic begins, then, when the Amazon woman has to face her suffering. This prompts her to develop a more intimate relationship with herself and the world. But that's too scary. So she takes another direction. First she moves in the direction of warmth and nurture, the Mother. If she finds a safe harbor and begins to feel nourished, she can by degrees plummet into her Medial Woman—becoming more involved in her own symbols, dreams and intuition. As she discovers the underground of herself, she feels stronger and more prepared, gradually moving toward the Hetaira, back into the world.

Of course this is very new and tough going for her, and her progress may be uneven. She will go forward and regress through many cycles in a lifetime. At the same time it doesn't behoove her to identify with the archetypes. These forces are alive in her psyche and help to let her know when she's been seized by one of them. As she makes these minute discoveries, she begins to ask herself if her action or compulsion serves her. Throughout her life she may have a tendency toward the Amazon in times of fear because it is her most developed side. But she has other sides too.

With each major loss, World Weary Woman prefers reenacting the Amazon. When such busyness runs its course, her suffering brings her to the necessity of the Mother. When accompaniment provides sufficient warmth and safe support, she descends into the domain of the Medial Woman. Here she is schooled in the eternal mysteries requisite for deeper relatedness. As her development continues, she ascends from the depths and returns to what her "curriculum" requires of her in the outer world of intimate partnership.

As life would have it, another growth challenge then surfaces, drawing her back to her dominant home base, the Amazon. As her personality matures, there is increased integration of the four feminine types, and enhanced fluidity. While each of these archetypes expresses itself differently through her, they seem to offer a means of relating to her unknown nature in more intimate ways. World Weary Woman's encounter with these archetypal ways of functioning provides the opportunity to differentiate who she is, disentangling from over-identification with any one of them. Once she finds herself in their field, she can, with dedication, discern the difference between her personal experience of the moment and the collective expectation.

It is this truth, in part, which sets her free.

Bibliography

Adler, Gerhard. "Remembering and Forgetting." Panarion Conference Los Angeles: The Panarion Foundation, 1976.

Barker, Culver M. *Healing in Depth.* London: Hodder and Stoughton. 1972.

Biedermann, Hans. *Dictionary of Symbolism.* New York: Facts On File, Inc., 1992.

Cather, Willa. *The Song of the Lark.* Boston: Houghton Mifflin Company, 1967.

Cirlot, J.E. *A Dictionary of Symbols.* New York: Barnes and Noble, 1995.

Copland, Aaron. *Music and Imagination.* London: Oxford University Press, 1952.

Crawford, Dan. *Back to the Long Grass.* London: Hodder and Stoughton, 1924.

Douglass, B., and Moustakas, C. "Heuristic Inquiry: The internal search to know." In *Journal of Human. Psychology,* vol. 25, no. 3 (July 1985).

Durkheim, Emile. *The Elementary Forms of the Religious Life.* New York: Oxford University Press, 1965.

Edinger, Edward. F. *The Creation of Consciousness: Jung's Myth for Modern Man.* Toronto: Inner City Books, 1984.

Elder, George R., ed. *The Body: An Encyclopedia of Archetypal Symbolism.* Boston: Shambhala, 1996.

Erikson, Eric. *Identity.* London: Faber and Faber, 1968.

Fleming, Anne T. *Motherhood Deferred. A Woman's Journey.* New York: G. P. Putnam's Sons, 1994.

Frankl, Viktor. *Man's Search For Meaning.* New York: Washington Square Press, 1984.

Freud, Anna. *The Ego and the Mechanisms of Defense.* London: The Hogarth Press and the Institute of Psycho-Analysis, 1968.

Freud, Sigmund. "An Autobiographical Study." In *Standard Edition,* vol. XX. London: The Hogarth Press and The Institute of Psycho-Analysis, 1959.

________. *Totem and Taboo.* London: Oxford University Press, 1950.

Friedman, Morris. *Pathogenesis of Coronary Artery Disease.* New York: McGraw-Hill, 1969.

Friedman, Meyer, and Rosenman, Ray. *Type A Behavior and Your Heart.* New York: Knopf, 1974.

Gardner, Howard. *Art, Mind, and Brain: A Cognitive Approach to Creativity.* New York: Basic Books, 1982.

Gendlin, Eugene. *Focusing.* New York: Bantam Books, 1998.

Grahn, Judy. *Blood, Bread, and Roses.* Boston: Beacon Press, 1993.

Grimm Brothers. *The Complete Grimms' Fairy Tales.* New York: Pantheon Books, 1944.

Grollman, Earl. *Talking About Death.* Boston: Beacon Press, 1970.

Hartdegen, Stephen, and Obstat, Hihil, eds. *The New American Bible.* New York: Catholic Book Publishing Co., 1991

Hildegard of Bingen. *Illuminations of Hildegard of Bingen.* Commentary by Matthew Fox. Santa Fe: Bear & Company, 1985.

Jacobsohn, Helmuth, ed. *The Dialogue of a World-Weary Man with His Ba.* Evanston, IL: Northwestern University Press, 1968.

Jewett, C.L. *Helping Children Cope with Separation and Loss.* Cambridge, MA: Harvard Common Press, 1982.

Jung, C.G. *The Collected Works* (Bollingen Series XX). 20 vols. Trans. R.F.C. Hull. Ed. H. Read, M. Fordham, G. Adler, Wm. McGuire. Princeton: Princeton University Press, 1953-1979.

________. *C.G. Jung Letters* (Bollingen Series XCV). 2 vols. Trans. R.F.C. Hull. Ed. Gerhard Adler and Aniela Jaffé. Princeton University Press, Princeton, 1973.

________. *Memories, Dreams, Reflections.* New York: Vintage Books, 1965.

Jung, C.G., and Kerényi, Karl. *Essays on a Science of Mythology.* Princeton: Princeton University Press, 1993.

Kellogue, Rhoda. *Analyzing Children's Art.* Mountain View, CA: Mayfield Publishing, 1970.

Kushner, Harold. *When Bad Things Happen to Good People.* New York: Avon Books, 1983.

Lewis, C.S. *A Grief Observed.* New York: Bantam Books, 1976.

Luke, Helen. *Woman: Earth and Spirit.* New York: Crossroad, 1993.

________. *The Way of Woman.* New York: Bantam Doubleday, 1995.

Maguire, Anne. "The Relationship Between the Unconscious Psyche and the Organ of the Skin." In *Harvest,* vol. 18 (1972)

Masson, Jeffrey M,, and McCarthy, Susan. *When Elephants Weep: The Emotional Lives of Animals.* New York: Delacorte Press (Bantam), 1995.

May, Rollo. *The Power to Create.* New York: Bantam Books, 1985.

Metzner, Ralph. *The Well of Remembrance.* Boston: Shambhala, 1994.

Neumann, Erich. *The Child.* Trans. Ralph Manheim. Boston: Shambhala, 1990.

________. *History and Origins of Consciousness* (Bollingen Series XLII). Princeton: Princeton University Press, 1973.

Pagels, Elaine. *The Gnostic Gospels.* New York: Vintage Books, 1989.

Peat, David F. *Infinite Potential: The Life and Times of David Bohm.* Reading, MA: Helix Books, 1997.

Pitzele, Peter. *Our Fathers' Wells.* San Francisco: Harper Collins, 1995.

Radin, Paul. *The World of Primitive Man.* Schuman: New York, 1952.

Stern, Harold. *The Interpersonal World of the Infant.* New York: Harper, 1984.

Stevens, Anthony. *Archetypes: A Natural History of the Self.* New York: William Morrow, 1982.

Storr, Anthony. *The Dynamics of Creation.* New York: Ballantine Books, 1993.

Van der Post, Laurens. *About Blady: A Pattern Out of Time.* New York: William Morrow, 1992.

________. *Jung and the Story of Our Time.* New York: Pantheon Books, 1975.

Ventura, Michael. *Shadow Dancing in the U.S.A.* New York: St. Martin's Press, 1985.

Von Franz, Marie-Louise. *Alchemical Active Imagination.* Irving, TX: Spring Publications, 1979.

Walker, Barbara. *The Woman's Encyclopedia Of Myths And Secrets.* San Francisco: Harper and Row, 1983.

Wilhelm, Richard. *The Secret of the Golden Flower.* London: Harcourt Brace Jovanovich, 1962.

Wilhelm, Richard, and Baynes, Cary. *The I Ching, or Book Of Changes* (Bollingen Series XIX). Princeton: Princeton University Press, 1967.

Wolff, Toni. "Structural Forms of the Feminine Psyche." Trans. Paul Watzlawik. C.G. Jung Institute, Zurich: Privately Printed, 1985.

Woodman, Marion. *Addiction to Perfection: The Still Unravished Bride.* Toronto: Inner City Books, 1982

________. *The Pregnant Virgin: A Process of Psychological Transformation.* Toronto: Inner City Books, 1985.

Index

Studies in Jungian Psychology by Jungian Analysts

Quality Paperbacks

Prices and payment in $US (except in Canada, $Cdn)

1. The Secret Raven: Conflict and Transformation
Daryl Sharp (Toronto). ISBN 0-919123-00-7. 128 pp. $16

2. The Psychological Meaning of Redemption Motifs in Fairy Tales
Marie-Louise von Franz (Zürich). ISBN 0-919123-01-5. 128 pp. $16

3. On Divination and Synchronicity: The Psychology of Meaningful Chance
Marie-Louise von Franz (Zürich). ISBN 0-919123-02-3. 128 pp. $16

4. The Owl Was a Baker's Daughter: Obesity, Anorexia and the Repressed Feminine Marion Woodman (Toronto). ISBN 0-919123-03-1. 144 pp. $16

5. Alchemy: An Introduction to the Symbolism and the Psychology
Marie-Louise von Franz (Zürich). ISBN 0-919123-04-X. 288 pp. $20

6. Descent to the Goddess: A Way of Initiation for Women
Sylvia Brinton Perera (New York). ISBN 0-919123-05-8. 112 pp. $16

7. The Psyche as Sacrament: A Comparative Study of C.G. Jung and Paul Tillich John P. Dourley (Ottawa). ISBN 0-919123-06-6. 128 pp. $16

8. Border Crossings: Carlos Castaneda's Path of Knowledge
Donald Lee Williams (Boulder). ISBN 0-919123-07-4. 160 pp. $16

9. Narcissism and Character Transformation: The Psychology of Narcissistic Character Disorders
Nathan Schwartz-Salant (New York). ISBN 0-919123-08-2. 192 pp. $18

10. Rape and Ritual: A Psychological Study
Bradley A. Te Paske (Santa Barbara). ISBN 0-919123-09-0. 160 pp. $16

11. Alcoholism and Women: The Background and the Psychology
Jan Bauer (Montreal). ISBN 0-919123-10-4. 144 pp. $16

12. Addiction to Perfection: The Still Unravished Bride
Marion Woodman (Toronto). ISBN 0-919123-11-2. 208 pp. $18pb/$25hc

13. Jungian Dream Interpretation: A Handbook of Theory and Practice
James A. Hall, M.D. (Dallas). ISBN 0-919123-12-0. 128 pp. $16

14. The Creation of Consciousness: Jung's Myth for Modern Man
Edward F. Edinger (Los Angeles). ISBN 0-919123-13-9. 128 pp. $16

15. The Analytic Encounter: Transference and Human Relationship
Mario Jacoby (Zürich). ISBN 0-919123-14-7. 128 pp. $16

16. Change of Life: Dreams and the Menopause
Ann Mankowitz (Ireland). ISBN 0-919123-15-5. 128 pp. $16

17. The Illness That We Are: A Jungian Critique of Christianity
John P. Dourley (Ottawa). ISBN 0-919123-16-3. 128 pp. $16

18. Hags and Heroes: A Feminist Approach to Jungian Psychotherapy with Couples Polly Young-Eisendrath (Philadelphia). ISBN 0-919123-17-1. 192 pp. $18

19. Cultural Attitudes in Psychological Perspective
Joseph L. Henderson, M.D. (San Francisco). ISBN 0-919123-18-X. 128 pp. $16

20. The Vertical Labyrinth: Individuation in Jungian Psychology
Aldo Carotenuto (Rome). ISBN 0-919123-19-8. 144 pp. $16

21. The Pregnant Virgin: A Process of Psychological Transformation
Marion Woodman (Toronto). ISBN 0-919123-20-1. 208 pp. $18pb/$25hc

22. Encounter with the Self: A Jungian Commentary on William Blake's *Illustrations of the Book of Job*
Edward F. Edinger (Los Angeles). ISBN 0-919123-21-X. 80 pp. $15

23. The Scapegoat Complex: Toward a Mythology of Shadow and Guilt
Sylvia Brinton Perera (New York). ISBN 0-919123-22-8. 128 pp. $16

24. The Bible and the Psyche: Individuation Symbolism in the Old Testament
Edward F. Edinger (Los Angeles). ISBN 0-919123-23-6. 176 pp. $18

25. The Spiral Way: A Woman's Healing Journey
Aldo Carotenuto (Rome). ISBN 0-919123-24-4. 144 pp. $16

26. The Jungian Experience: Analysis and Individuation
James A. Hall, M.D. (Dallas). ISBN 0-919123-25-2. 176 pp. $18

27. Phallos: Sacred Image of the Masculine
Eugene Monick (Scranton, PA). ISBN 0-919123-26-0. 144 pp. $16

28. The Christian Archetype: A Jungian Commentary on the Life of Christ
Edward F. Edinger (Los Angeles). ISBN 0-919123-27-9. 144 pp. $16

29. Love, Celibacy and the Inner Marriage
John P. Dourley (Ottawa). ISBN 0-919123-28-7. 128 pp. $16

30. Touching: Body Therapy and Depth Psychology
Deldon Anne McNeely (Lynchburg, VA). ISBN 0-919123-29-5. 128 pp. $16

31. Personality Types: Jung's Model of Typology
Daryl Sharp (Toronto). ISBN 0-919123-30-9. 128 pp. $16

32. The Sacred Prostitute: Eternal Aspect of the Feminine
Nancy Qualls-Corbett (Birmingham). ISBN 0-919123-31-7. 176 pp. $18

33. When the Spirits Come Back
Janet O. Dallett (Seal Harbor, WA). ISBN 0-919123-32-5. 160 pp. $16

34. The Mother: Archetypal Image in Fairy Tales
Sibylle Birkhäuser-Oeri (Zürich). ISBN 0-919123-33-3. 176 pp. $18

35. The Survival Papers: Anatomy of a Midlife Crisis
Daryl Sharp (Toronto). ISBN 0-919123-34-1. 160 pp. $16

36. The Cassandra Complex: Living with Disbelief
Laurie Layton Schapira (New York). ISBN 0-919123-35-X. 160 pp. $16

37. Dear Gladys: The Survival Papers, Book 2
Daryl Sharp (Toronto). ISBN 0-919123-36-8. 144 pp. $16

38. The Phallic Quest: Priapus and Masculine Inflation
James Wyly (Chicago). ISBN 0-919123-37-6. 128 pp. $16

39. Acrobats of the Gods: Dance and Transformation
Joan Dexter Blackmer (Wilmot Flat, NH). ISBN 0-919123-38-4. 128 pp. $16

40. Eros and Pathos: Shades of Love and Suffering
Aldo Carotenuto (Rome). ISBN 0-919123-39-2. 160 pp. $16

41. The Ravaged Bridegroom: Masculinity in Women
Marion Woodman (Toronto). ISBN 0-919123-42-2. 224 pp. $20

42. Liberating the Heart: Spirituality and Jungian Psychology
Lawrence W. Jaffe (Berkeley). ISBN 0-919123-43-0. 176 pp. $18

43. Goethe's *Faust:* Notes for a Jungian Commentary
Edward F. Edinger (Los Angeles). ISBN 0-919123-44-9. 112 pp. $16

44. The Dream Story
Donald Broadribb (Baker's Hill, Australia). ISBN 0-919123-45-7. 256 pp. $20

45. The Rainbow Serpent: Bridge to Consciousness
Robert L. Gardner (Toronto). ISBN 0-919123-46-5. 128 pp. $16

46. Circle of Care: Clinical Issues in Jungian Therapy
Warren Steinberg (New York). ISBN 0-919123-47-3. 160 pp. $16

47. Jung Lexicon: A Primer of Terms & Concepts
Daryl Sharp (Toronto). ISBN 0-919123-48-1. 160 pp. $16

48. Body and Soul: The Other Side of Illness
Albert Kreinheder (Los Angeles). ISBN 0-919123-49-X. 112 pp. $16

49. Animus Aeternus: Exploring the Inner Masculine
Deldon Anne McNeely (Lynchburg, VA). ISBN 0-919123-50-3. 192 pp. $18

50. Castration and Male Rage: The Phallic Wound
Eugene Monick (Scranton, PA). ISBN 0-919123-51-1. 144 pp. $16

51. Saturday's Child: Encounters with the Dark Gods
Janet O. Dallett (Seal Harbor, WA). ISBN 0-919123-52-X. 128 pp. $16

52. The Secret Lore of Gardening: Patterns of Male Intimacy
Graham Jackson (Toronto). ISBN 0-919123-53-8. 160 pp. $16

53. The Refiner's Fire: Memoirs of a German Girlhood
Sigrid R. McPherson (Los Angeles). ISBN 0-919123-54-6. 208 pp. $18

54. Transformation of the God-Image: Jung's *Answer to Job*
Edward F. Edinger (Los Angeles). ISBN 0-919123-55-4. 144 pp. $16

55. Getting to Know You: The Inside Out of Relationship
Daryl Sharp (Toronto). ISBN 0-919123-56-2. 128 pp. $16

56. A Strategy for a Loss of Faith: Jung's Proposal
John P. Dourley (Ottawa). ISBN 0-919123-57-0. 144 pp. $16

57. Close Relationships: Family, Friendship, Marriage
Eleanor Bertine (New York). ISBN 0-919123-58-9. 160 pp. $16

58. Conscious Femininity: Interviews with Marion Woodman
Introduction by Marion Woodman (Toronto). ISBN 0-919123-59-7. 160 pp. $16

59. The Middle Passage: From Misery to Meaning in Midlife
James Hollis (Houston). ISBN 0-919123-60-0. 128 pp. $16

60. The Living Room Mysteries: Patterns of Male Intimacy, Book 2
Graham Jackson (Toronto). ISBN 0-919123-61-9. 144 pp. $16

61. Chicken Little: The Inside Story *(A Jungian Romance)*
Daryl Sharp (Toronto). ISBN 0-919123-62-7. 128 pp. $16

62. Coming To Age: The Croning Years and Late-Life Transformation
Jane R. Prétat (Providence, RI). ISBN 0-919123-63-5. 144 pp. $16

63. Under Saturn's Shadow: The Wounding and Healing of Men
James Hollis (Houston). ISBN 0-919123-64-3. 144 pp. $16

Discounts: *any 3-5 books, 10%; 6-9 books, 20%; 10 or more, 25%*
Add Postage/Handling: 1-2 books, $3; 3-4 books, $5; 5-9 books, $10; 10 or more, free

Write or phone for free Catalogue of **over 90 titles** and **Jung at Heart** newsletter

INNER CITY BOOKS

Box 1271, Station Q, Toronto, ON M4T 2P4, Canada **(416) 927-0355**